PRAISE FOR *Hiking Naked*

"For anyone yearning to change the way they live and work, *Hiking Naked* offers one woman's experience of following God's guidance and her own deepest wisdom, even in the midst of uncertainty and loss."
—EILEEN FLANAGAN, author of *Renewable: One Woman's Search for Simplicity, Faithfulness, and Hope*

"In candid, lyrical prose, Iris Graville offers a story of optimism in the midst of disillusionment. Her courageous spirit and unforgettable experiences may just inspire you to embark upon an adventure of your own."   —MELISSA HART, author of *Wild Within*

"As I navigate my own way through life, *Hiking Naked* gives me a sense of companionship with its amazing example of faithful living."
—KATHY RUNYAN, Co-Director, Ben Lomond Quaker Center

"I am grateful for Iris Graville's naked memoir—such revealing stories as herein contained provide light and hope—both much needed in a time such as ours."
—J. BRENT BILL, Quaker minister, author of *Holy Silence: The Gift of Quaker Spirituality*

"We need more stories like this, that reveal how we all can be guided by holy wisdom from within, if we take the time to listen and have the courage to follow where it leads."
—MARCELLE MARTIN, author of *Our Life is Love: The Quaker Spiritual Journey*

"Reading this tender, honest  memoir is
spending time with your wis   arm

"Reading this calm, contemp   l
bit like taking a long walk in ti.. .. .. a late Spring
day when the subalpine forest is starting to wake up, and you can
sense sap rising in the trees. It is on such a hike that you can look
into yourself and maybe hear a still, small voice. Listen to it."
—MARK ROZEMA, author of *Road Trip*

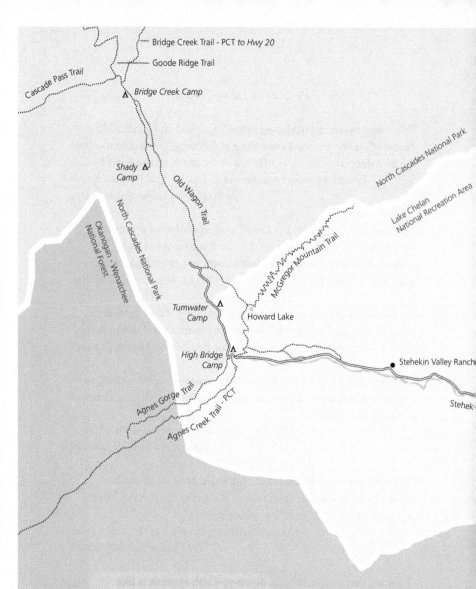

Bridge Creek Trail - PCT *to Hwy 20*

Goode Ridge Trail

Cascade Pass Trail

Bridge Creek Camp

Shady Camp

Old Wagon Trail

North Cascades National Park

Lake Chelan National Recreation Area

North Cascades National Park

Okanogan - Wenatchee National Forest

McGregor Mountain Trail

Tumwater Camp

Howard Lake

High Bridge Camp

Stehekin Valley Ranch

Agnes Gorge Trail

Agnes Creek Trail - PCT

Stehek

NATIONAL PARK SERVICE

WELCOME TO
STEHEKIN

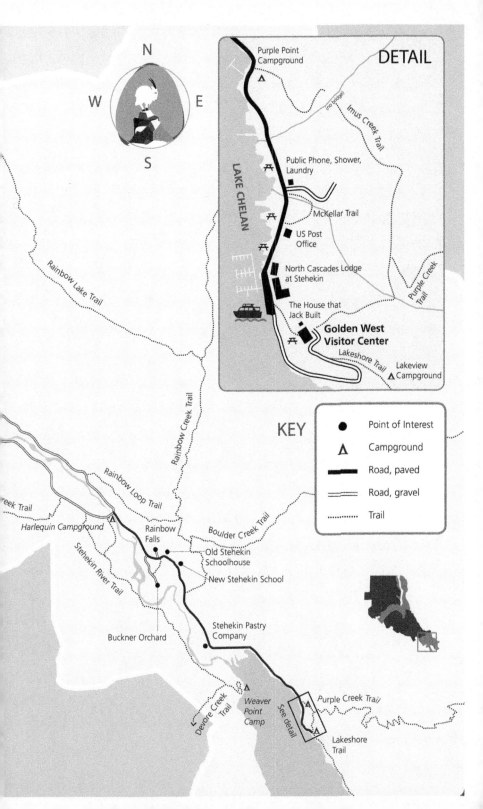

Hiking Naked

Hiking Naked

A Quaker Woman's Search for Balance

IRIS GRAVILLE

Homebound Publications
Ensuring that the mainstream isn't the only stream.

Published in 2017 • Homebound Publications
Front Cover Image © Nancy Barnhart
Cover and Interior Designed by Leslie M. Browning
Map Provided by National Park Service. Used with Permission.
ISBN • 978-1-938846-84-7
First Edition Trade Paperback

Homebound Publications
Ensuring the mainstream isn't the only stream.

10 9 8 7 6 5 4 3 2 1

Homebound Publications is committed to ecological stewardship. We greatly value the natural environment and invest in environmental conservation. Our books are printed on paper with chain of custody certification from the Forest Stewardship Council, Sustainable Forestry Initiative, and the Program for the Endorsement of Forest Certification.

Contents

CHAPTER I

Hiking Naked

A s I rounded what I hoped was the hike's final switchback, a clump of blue at the trail's edge drew my gaze beyond the dusty toes of my boots. A rumpled T-shirt rested on top of khaki shorts and boxers; beside the clothes, a large pair of hiking boots. My eyes glided up past the boot's red laces, the dusty wool socks, the hairy legs. My husband, Jerry, struck a regal pose, one hand on his walking stick, the other on his naked hip. He gazed off into the distance, his chin up-turned, his mouth curved into a smile. "Want to hike with me to the lookout?" he said.

Just the night before, we'd sat around our fire at Harlequin Campground in the tiny village of Stehekin, Washington. Jerry had read out loud from a guidebook about today's hike on the

I

Goode Ridge Trail. He'd pronounced it good-ee, the way the
locals did, even though its namesake, topographer Richard U.
G-o-o-d-e, pronounced it Good. Since this August vacation
was our only chance all year to hike, the Goode Trail seemed a
good place to start.

I'm sure Jerry had read me the entire entry about the hike
to Goode Ridge, including the part about five thousand feet of
elevation gain in five miles. What I'd remembered as we set off
this morning, though, was the promise that the top was level
with a 360-degree panoramic view of Goode Mountain, Trap-
per Lake, McGregor Mountain, Glacier Peak, and the Stehekin Valley. What I had forgotten was the guidebook's rating of
the hike as "strenuous" and the description of the trail going up
"steeply and remorselessly in woods with few views for the first
2.5 miles."

An hour-and-a-half into the hike, I sounded like our kids at
the start of a long car trip.

"Jer, how much farther?"

"Not too much. We're about half-way there."

"Half-way?"

"Yeah…but you've done the hardest part. How about some
more water?"

I chugged a third of my water bottle's contents, then moist-
ened my cotton bandana to wipe my sweaty neck. Jerry stood
beside where I'd slumped down onto a smooth boulder; he
reached for my hand. "We'll be there before you know it," he
said, pulling me to my feet. Momentarily refreshed, I breathed
in the spicy scent I'd notice on every visit to Lake Chelan and
the Stehekin Valley. I wouldn't know for many years, though,
that the smell was from *ceanothus*, a shrub with shiny green
leaves that colonizes areas after forest fires. Then, I just knew
that the whiff stirred feelings that I was in my true home.

*   *   *

STEHEKIN, TRANSLATED AS "THE WAY THROUGH," once was a passageway for Skagit and Salish Indians through the North Cascades of Washington State. Later, highways were blasted through parts of the mountain range along Lake Chelan, but none of them ever made it the lake's fifty-five-mile length to the community at the end. Today, a more accurate description of Stehekin might be "the way away."

Like us, most people get "uplake" on *The Lady of the Lake*, a commercial, passenger-only ferry that makes one trip daily in the summer. The Lady sails four times a week in spring and fall, but in the winter, it runs only on Monday, Wednesday, and Friday. Depending on whether you catch the boat at the lake's midway mark at Fields Point or at its beginning in the town of Chelan, it takes two-and-a-half to four hours to reach Stehekin. Some opt for a half-hour floatplane ride; the hardy hike a full day over National Park and Forest Service trails. Telephone lines from the "downlake" world never made it to Stehekin, and there still aren't any cell towers, either. Most interaction among Stehekin's eighty year-round residents takes place face-to-face. Contact with the rest of the world is by mail and now, for those who have satellite dishes, by e-mail. A single public telephone, for outgoing calls only, haltingly relays voices via satellite when communication is urgent.

*   *   *

AFTER PASSING THE HALFWAY POINT, we hiked on without talking, the trail worshipful. Soon, we glimpsed the glacial blue of Bridge Creek, nearly a thousand feet below. Several switchbacks later, we sighted jagged ridges, carved by 180-million-year-old glaciers that seemed within an arm's reach; the blue-gray shadows of dozens more marched for miles toward the horizon. As we paused, I said a silent prayer of thanks for this time in this place.

Here, every summer since 1983, a weeklong vacation alone with Jerry had given me needed times of quiet. With our twin son and daughter, Matt and Rachel, in the care of Jerry's folks in Oregon, the solitude and the slowed pace helped me open to the spiritual voice I relied on for guidance. At home, it was muffled too often by taxiing the kids to school, soccer practice, and the orthodontist; by worries about the mortgage and the grocery bills; and by frustration with my work as a public health nurse. This year, during our ninth return to the mountains, I needed the escape as much as ever.

Most Sundays throughout the year, Jerry and I sat in silence for an hour at our Quaker Meeting in the college town of Bellingham, Washington. Rachel and Matt, now ten years old, would hang out with the only other child who came to Meeting and an adult volunteer in a room set up as kids' space. I'd breathe in deeply and count silently to ten as I tried to empty my mind to listen for what Quakers call "the still, small voice." I knew that single hour on Sunday wasn't enough to keep me centered, but I rarely managed to squeeze out any minutes during the week to reconnect with the Spirit that sustained me. Here in the wilderness, I was hoping to make up for lost time—and connection.

As the trail re-entered the woods and zigzagged steeply, my thoughts started to roil. I couldn't remain quiet any longer, and words tumbled. I was a failure in my job. Was I doing what I was meant to do? Jerry, just slightly ahead of me, offered supportive comments and alerted me to mountain peaks visible at spots where the forest opened up. How many times in our dozen years together had he bolstered me as I wrestled with childhood losses, conflicts with my mom, and long-standing fears that I wasn't good enough? Though I was weary of re-playing those old tapes, I was at it again. And once again, he listened. Eventually, the trail's upward course stole the air from my complaints; I shifted my focus to the cramps in my calves and the weight on my back.

"Now how far?" I had asked then, as Jerry's blue T-shirt and khaki hiking shorts disappeared around a switchback.

"Uh, just about a mile-and-a-half," he called back over his shoulder.

Head down and shoulders hunched, I willed my feet for-ward. "Dammit," I said out loud, as a tree root snagged my shuf-fling steps. *One-and-a-half miles more,* I thought. *I can't wimp out... but I don't know if I can do it.* All I could see were rocks and pinecones sputtering from under my boots as I shambled along, far outpaced by marmots darting between boulders. *Just keep putting one foot in front of the other,* I coached myself. *It'll be worth it when you get to the top.*

When I couldn't hear Jerry's footsteps anymore, I figured he was already at the summit, taking in the view of all those peaks listed in the guidebook. Instead, he was silently disrobing.

I couldn't help but laugh out loud at Jerry's naked pose as I scanned the trail ahead and behind for signs of other hikers who might happen upon this unexpected sight. This was one of the reasons I'd married this man. His playfulness once again helped me move forward, fully clothed, but with my spirit lightened. In the coming years, I'd retell this story to family and countless friends with the same glee, and gratitude, I felt that moment on the trail.

A few minutes later, with Jerry back in shorts and T-shirt and at my side at that level ridge top the guidebook had promised, I took in the sweep of mountains, river, lake, and valley. For now, the ache in my quads—and my heart—eased. I wouldn't realize until a few years later that the trek to Goode Ridge was the start of my journey to regain the spiritual footing I'd lost. At times I would feel that I was the one who was hiking naked.

CHAPTER 2

Singed

BACK IN BELLINGHAM AFTER OUR WEEK IN STEHEKIN, slip-on clogs replaced my hiking boots. As I climbed the stairs to my client's second floor apartment, angry voices seeped into the hallway. So did the stench of cigarette smoke. My blue canvas bag, bulging with handouts about pregnancy and mother-infant interactions, dug into my shoulder as I searched for a file folder. After my first knock on the thin door, a high-pitched burst outshouted the quarrelling voices.

"Turn the goddamn TV down, Joey. The nurse is here."

And here I was, once again face-to-face with this twenty-year-old—more girl than woman—a toddler straddling her hip, his thigh gripped by her hand that held a cigarette sending up a curl of smoke. Her T-shirt strained over the curve of her pregnancy. She turned toward the little boy kneeling inches from the soap opera on the television screen.

"Joey, what did I just say? Turn it down!"

Her pale blonde hair swung as she twisted toward the boy, and I could see a bruise on her cheek.

My heart sank then, just as it had the day before when her referral had shown up on my desk at the county health department. The prenatal clinic report said she was pregnant again, a third baby on the way with the same man who had fathered the first two—the same man who had sent her to the hospital more than once with bruises and broken bones. I worked my mouth into a smile as I entered the one-bedroom apartment. I didn't realize then that the beginnings of burnout had singed both my compassion and my passion for my work.

I had felt called to nursing while in high school, although I didn't use that terminology at the time and, until the first day of my senior year in high school, I'd been heading on another path.

"Did you hear Patti got accepted to Deaconess School of Nursing?" a friend had asked while we took our flutes out of their cases during second period band.

"But she never took chemistry," I said. "I didn't think you could get into nursing school without chemistry."

"Well, Deaconess let her in without it."

Memories of my mom's hospitalization six years earlier for a benign brain tumor flooded me. As an eleven-year-old, I'd idolized the nursing students in their crisp white pinafores with shiny bandage scissors snug in their waistbands, their spotless, white nursing oxfords squeaking as they walked the polished floors of the hospital hallways. To be like them, though, I figured I'd have to study chemistry and physics in high school, taught by the rigid Miss Tennes. Fearing she'd destroy my straight-A average, I denied a lingering interest in nursing.

In an instant, though, and with just that one piece of information about Patti, I admitted to myself that nursing, not an English degree, was what I really wanted. I stopped in the counselor's office that afternoon, picked up an application for Deaconess, a three-year hospital-based nursing program, and went to work on it that night. A few weeks later, I learned that Deaconess didn't mind that I hadn't studied chemistry either, and along with Patti, I started nursing school in the fall. Eventually, I came to view that conversation during band warm-up as one of those mystical moments when something outside of me gave me a shove.

I first heard the term "burnout" not long after graduating from nursing school in 1974, the same year that psychotherapist Herbert Freudenberger coined the term in his book, *Burnout: The High Cost of High Achievement*. He wrote of the depletion felt by people in the "caring professions"— teaching, social work, nursing.

At that same time, nurse and researcher Marlene Kramer published *Reality Shock: Why Nurses Leave Nursing*. Her study showed that new nurses weren't prepared for the realities of the emotional and physical demands of their profession once they left the supportive environment of their nursing programs.

But burnout and reality shock had been only phrases in books for me back when I became a registered nurse. Then, I tucked my blonde ponytail under a starched, box-shaped, white cap and pinned on a nametag that read *Miss S. Northcote, RN*, for my first job in 3-ICU, the ten-bed intensive care unit at Indiana University Medical Center. The "S" stood for a name that I'd received by default. Supposedly, my parents couldn't agree, so my father settled it by telling everyone at work that his new daughter was named Stacey. Now, barely twenty-one years old, I was taking care of men my dad's age—men fresh from quadruple artery grafts to repair their stressed hearts. I suctioned tracheotomies of smokers whose cancer had invaded their throats and voice boxes. And I cleaned the diarrhea stools of four-hundred-pound patients after surgeries to bypass their small intestines.

As a new graduate, I chose ICU because there I could give total care, doing everything for my patient—bathing; mixing intravenous fluids; measuring body fluids from the chest, bladder, and stomach; cleaning incisions and changing dressings; monitoring vital signs. When things went well, they went very well.

One afternoon, I ushered a woman into her husband's ICU room half an hour after his open-heart surgery. Color drained from her face as she gazed at her husband's motionless body. A monitor chimed each beat of his heart, and a ventilator clicked with each breath. The air held the smell of the iodine antiseptic painted around his incision that stretched from nipple line to pubic bone.

I explained the green squiggles on the heart monitor screen, the tubes draining blood from her husband's chest cavity and urine from his bladder, and how the ventilator pushed oxygen into his windpipe through the tube protruding from his mouth. At that moment, she was as much my patient as her husband was.

"He looks so sick," she said.

"I know," I said, "but soon he'll be breathing on his own and sitting up. You'll be amazed."

And within two days, like most open-heart patients, he did breathe on his own, sipped juices, took a few steps, and was moved to a surgical ward. A few days after that he went home, and I was nursing another patient and family through this cycle of near-death and recovery.

When things went bad in ICU, though, they were very bad. Like the man in his twenties I was assigned to one night, his aorta severed in a motorcycle accident. All night after his surgery, I hung bag after bag of whole blood to replace what had been lost; his shaky vital signs signaled blood was still seeping from his damaged heart. Every hour, his mother came in for the ten-minute visit we allowed.

"Is that more blood you're giving?" she asked, as I put a bag on an IV pole.

I nodded.

"How much has he had?"

I flipped through the notebook on the bedside stand where I recorded each unit of blood. I took a deep breath to steady my voice. "This is his fourth."

She dropped her chin to her chest and cried softly. A few hours later, her son's heart gave out. Alone in the room, preparing it for the next patient, I pitched depleted blood bags into the garbage, wadded up blood-spattered disposable bed pads, and yanked the edges of fresh sheets into tight corners over the mattress. My tears would flow, later, in the quiet of my apartment.

After a year, I tired of the focus on machines, tired of hearing ventilator alarms in my sleep, and longed for patients who were conscious and mobile. Studies show that young nurses are more vulnerable than older professionals to burnout, but I denied that as my source of fatigue. Instead, I justified my resignation from ICU with my decision to move back to Evansville, Indiana, where I'd earned my nursing diploma, to study full-time for a bachelor's degree in nursing. The university program required community health, and I found in that specialty a way to bring together my desire to promote health and to provide care for the poor and underserved. After finishing my degree, I went to work for the local Visiting Nurse Association.

When I worked in the hospital, I couldn't fully know what my patients were going home to when they were discharged. As a home health nurse, though, I cared for them in their own bedrooms and sat with them at their kitchen tables to count out doses for their pill containers. Instead of a sterile exam room, I escorted them to their living rooms to check blood pressure and listen to their lungs. Elderly patients told stories of the children and grandchildren whose framed photographs lined fireplace mantles and bookshelves.

Phillip, one patient in my inner city caseload, had been referred for help to administer antibiotic eye drops. I wasn't sure his reddened, watering blue eyes could see me when he met me at the door. I cleared stacks of dirty dishes from the kitchen table to make room for my black leather visiting nurse bag and washed my hands at the coffee-stained porcelain sink. Phillip sat at the table, his toothless mouth gumming a hunk of white bread.

"I'm just going to wipe your eyes with these wet cotton balls before I put in the medicine," I said, dabbing at puddles of yellow drainage in the corners of Phillip's eyes.

"Humph," he grunted.

"Where are your eye drops?"

"In the fridge," he growled, jerking his head toward a dingy-white model. The handle wobbled as I opened the door, and I noticed the air inside the refrigerator was only slightly cooler than the summer afternoon temperature. As I reached for the medicine bottle on a rusty shelf, a cockroach skittered out the door onto the floor. I took a few steps back, slightly grossed out, but also feeling a tad smug. Here, in patients' homes, far from the orderly, sterile hospital environment, I dealt with their realities.

By then, five years into my nursing career, private corporations had started to run hospitals, and I was glad to be out of a system where I saw that profit trumped care. I feared the non-profit VNA would be the next to shift. How long would it be before Medicare would deny funding for my visits to a nearly-blind man with cockroaches in his refrigerator, justifying their refusal as a way to increase cost-effectiveness? I assumed the public health system would survive as the safety net to catch those who would fall through the inevitable cracks, and I wanted to learn more about how to influence health policy. Jerry and I had married the year before, and he and I moved to Seattle so I could attend graduate school at the University of Washington. Those burnout experts might have viewed my return to school as an escape from the emotional demands of caring for people like Phillip, but I saw it as a way to help even more.

Three years later, now a parent of twins and with a new master's degree in hand, I focused my nursing practice on pregnant women and children. As the nurse in a center for abused and neglected children, I worked side-by-side with childcare providers, social workers, and speech therapists to create a safe and healthy haven—at least for the six hours every weekday that the children were in our care.

"How do you deal with seeing all those abused kids?" many people asked when I told them about my job. In the early days, I'd say this role was a way I could impact children's lives, possibly prevent some of the desperate situations of the adults in my previous visiting nurse caseload. I'd explain that the rewards of seeing undernourished infants and toddlers gain weight and overcome developmental delays eased the heartbreak of their bruises, broken bones, cigarette-burned skin, and battered self-esteem. At the end of each workday, I hugged my own two pre-schoolers a little longer.

Three years after starting at the child care center, I resigned to take a job in public health policy with the State Department of Health. I again rationalized my job change as a way to make a difference for more children and their caregivers. To make that difference, though, I'd wake my own two children while it was still dark, buckle them into their car seats, and drive them to a childcare center when its doors opened at six-thirty a.m. There, the teacher helped me get Rachel and Matt, still in their pajamas, dressed and seated at child-sized tables and chairs for Cheerios and orange juice. More than once I left one or both of them sobbing as I hurried to a city parking lot to meet a Vanpool for an hour-long commute to the state capitol. I dragged home from work each day, snapped at Jerry and the kids, and groused about bureaucratic change at the pace of a banana slug. My march toward burnout was picking up speed.

My government position often took me around the state. On one trip north to Bellingham, I noticed cedars and firs sweeping up rocky slopes on one side of the roadway and Bellingham Bay rippling in the sunlight on the other. I could almost believe I was approaching our annual get-away in Stehekin. Within a year, Jerry would be hired as a classroom sign language interpreter at a Bellingham high school, and I'd convince my boss I could handle my statewide role from there. During our years in Seattle, we'd started attending Quaker meeting; there was one in Bellingham, too, adding even more to the appeal of this smaller community. We found a house to rent, and we enrolled the kids in a neighborhood elementary school. It was our first big move as a family, but not our last.

Two years after transplanting to Bellingham, discontent rose yet again. I felt too far removed from people in need, so I returned to direct patient care, this time at the county health department. We bought a house that was cycling distance to work for me and was a short bus ride to school for the kids. Weekday mornings, Jerry and I woke to the sound of Bob Edwards on National Public Radio's *Morning Edition*, we'd wake the kids, and the four of us would jockey around the kitchen making breakfast, packing lunches, and confirming after-school schedules. Depending on the season and the day of the week, we'd coordinate drop-off and pickup for soccer, gymnastics, or basketball. Still unaware of the searing effects of the emotional demands of nursing, I spent my workdays going to apartments like the one where Joey and his pregnant mom lived.

On Sundays at our small Quaker meeting, I'd spend the first moments of silent worship fidgeting in my chair and mentally creating a "to do" list for the coming week. I'd switch from one centering technique to another, most of them derailed by doubts about how, or whether, I could be of any help to women like Joey's mom. Now, eighteen years into my career as a nurse, and despite job changes and seeking clarity about how to regain the joy I'd once experienced in my work, the word "burnout" started to creep into my vocabulary. It wasn't what I'd imagined feeling as I was about to turn forty.

My co-worker, Peggy, achieved that milestone the year before me, and she marked it by inviting half a dozen women to join her in a Native American sweat lodge ceremony. I'd been drawn to Quakerism by the simplicity of worshiping in silence, without the rituals of confession, communion, hymn singing, and scripture reading I'd grown up with in the Lutheran church. I knew nothing of this practice Peggy had asked me to join in, but I wanted to support her. And as much as I resisted the notion that forty was "over the hill," I had to admit I was feeling vulnerable to it. I was intrigued by a practice that would honor this passage.

We gathered on a cool, June day in a secluded, forested spot not far from Bellingham. The leader of the sweat, a woman named Turtle, explained that over the next few hours we'd sit together inside a dome structure made of layer upon layer of wool blankets and heated by a fire she'd built in the center. Turtle pulled back the flap of wool that covered the opening, and we crawled across the dirt floor, our naked bodies beading with sweat as we moved in toward the heat. This was the first of four rounds that would each symbolize a different season as a metaphor for Peggy's transition into mid-life. I had gone in second, behind Peggy, ending up deep inside the tent, farthest from the opening. Once we were all inside, Turtle shut the flap, closing out air and light. I don't remember ever feeling so hot, or so in the dark.

As my body temperature climbed, I struggled to focus on Turtle's stories about seasons and stages of life. The word "iris" broke into my thoughts, then disappeared as I panted, trying to get enough air in my lungs to quash the feeling I was suffocating. I squinted at the glowing coals, searching for a bit of light. *Don't give in to your fear*, I thought. *Hang on until this round ends and you can go outside again.*

All I remember about the rest of the ceremony is the heat, the dark, the gulps of cool air I took outside the tent between rounds, and the return of "iris" during each round inside the tent. I ended the day in almost a dream-like state. Unexpectedly, on the drive home, I started to think of the word "iris" as a name. As *my* name.

I'd always envied people whose first names had meaning for them, but even though mine hadn't been passed down through my family or didn't have any cultural significance and seemed chosen casually, I'd never seriously considered changing it. Until that day in the sweat lodge with a big birthday just a year off.

That winter, I thumbed through flower bulb catalogs, admiring the range of colors and shapes of irises. I noticed that irises were depicted in art, literature, and mythology as symbols of beauty, strength, wisdom, and peace. I researched naming traditions and discovered that in many religions and cultures, people take new names at significant times of life. I practiced using the name Iris at a coffee shop or at one-time meetings with strangers. I liked the way it sounded with the last name of Graville that I'd adopted when Jerry and I married and with my middle name, Marie, which I shared with my mom and my maternal grandmother.

I worried that people would think taking a new first name was weird; I'd secretly reacted that way when I'd met Turtle at the sweat lodge. When I confided in a few friends about my plan, I was surprised to learn that several of them used names different from those they'd been given at birth. Even my mom had decided a few years earlier to go by Lee instead of her given name of Shirley. One night as I scooped ice cream into bowls for dessert, Jerry assured me he'd call me by this new name. The kids, now twelve, seemed unconcerned, too.

"We'll still call you Mom," Rachel said.

In the spring, I would pin on a different nametag at work, this one identifying me as *Iris Graville*. I might start a new decade with a new name, but I still didn't know what to do with my anger and frustration with the never-ending stream of families in need. As 1992 drew to a close, I tried to ease the sting of burnout by moving away from them and into middle management, adding a new title—Communicable Disease Supervisor—behind my name.

CHAPTER 3

Static and Signals

A N OUTBREAK OF E. COLI CONSUMED MY FIRST WEEKS as supervisor of the communicable disease program. With ten cases in the county of what was then, in January 1993, a new strain of the infection, the staff and I scrambled to keep up with directives from the state Department of Health and the Centers for Disease Control. When one of those patients—a two-year-old boy—died, we had to calm the fears of all of the families whose children attended the same childcare center.

The day after the child's death, I walked into my office, stepping around memos and faxes I'd stacked into piles on the floor. I moved mounds of paper off my chair and sat in the early morning quiet. Pink "While You Were Out" phone messages littered my desktop. My schedule for staffing the im-

‿n clinic poked out from under the previous day's *Seattle Times* with the headlines of E. coli incidence around the state. Young children were on respirators and in kidney failure as a result of this infection, and I still had to make sure we had nurses to give shots to the children who'd be filling our waiting room within an hour; the boxes on the calendar were shadowed with scribbles and white-out. In the following days, I juggled regional and national media and a public who no longer trusted they could eat a hamburger at their favorite fast food stop, all the while keeping our immunization and refugee clinics staffed and bringing in revenue. I was exhausted from the grief and worry that had robbed me of sleep for weeks.

Ten years after our first summer trip to Stehekin, I needed a respite there more than ever. A few years earlier we'd added a wintertime visit to the Valley, and that started a new tradition that included the kids. To them, Stehekin was always snow-covered. They spent entire days cross-country skiing and sledding; evenings, they'd read and play board games. We never heard them complain about the lack of television, movie theaters, or other basics of life in either Seattle or Bellingham.

In the absence of phones and still years away from Internet service, the valley hosted a robust grapevine. Through it we discovered that Wally Winkel, a long-time Stehekin bachelor, rented out his deceased mother's cabin at a reasonable monthly rate. Jerry's sign language interpreting job at a high school gave him the summer free, and with a combination of holidays, personal days, and vacation days, I could take most of a month off from work, too. We reserved Wally's cabin for that July, planning to return just after Rachel and Matt finished fifth grade. Throughout the rest of the winter and spring, the prospect of several weeks away from the health department kept me going as I faced ongoing challenges as a manager.

The kids took to summertime in Stehekin, joining us on bike rides to the bakery for its famous cinnamon rolls, hiking to Rainbow Falls, playing community softball, reading *Jurassic Park* out loud, playing Trivial Pursuit and card games, and greeting the boat when it brought visitors, freight, and the mail to the Stehekin Landing. Within a week, they felt at home enough to hang out with other Stehekin kids for a day of swimming in the lake while Jerry and I hiked to Agnes Gorge.

A warm, summer breeze and the flat, two-and-a-half mile trail loosened our knees and our dreams. With only three hundred feet of elevation gain, it was more of a stroll, surrounded by ponderosa pines, Douglas firs, and a small grove of aspens. Along the way, we paused for views of open hillside meadows and eight-thousand-foot Agnes Mountain. Stepping gingerly on rocks and fallen tree limbs to cross an icy stream cutting through the trail, we inhaled slower and more deeply than we had in months.

Just as we had on the hike to Goode Ridge a couple of years earlier, we began this gentler outing to Agnes Gorge daydreaming about living in Stehekin. We wondered aloud what it would be like without television or radio reception, without a grocery store or a daily newspaper. We talked of sending the kids to Stehekin's one-room school, with classmates of all ages from kindergarten through eighth grade and with the river and the forest as their playground. A school where reading and drawing, knitting and playing the recorder, writing and history and math and science were integrated with daily life.

Winding our way through the lush forest path, we fantasized about rising each day in the mountains and living in sync with the seasons and nature's rhythms. Jerry schemed about hikes into the backcountry whenever he wanted. I imagined

nighttimes so dark and silent I could not only see the stars
burst in the night sky but maybe hear them as well. Even July
and August temperatures in the upper nineties—a good twenty degrees hotter than summer days in Puget Sound—seemed
appealing, knowing that the glacier-fed Stehekin River would
cool us in an instant.

Sweating in the heat on that day's hike, we followed a ragged
offshoot at the end of the Agnes Trail down to a secluded spot
where we could skinny dip in the arctic-like river, the gorge's
fifteen-foot waterfall a backdrop. We whooped and giggled as
the water prickled our hot skin, then scrambled out to dry our
chilled bodies on sunbaked rocks. Back on the trail, as the last
refreshing water drops dried on my skin, my reflections shifted
to what awaited me back at work.

"I don't know if I'm cut out for management," I said. Puffs
of brown dust swirled around the toes of my hiking boots.

"You're a natural leader," Jerry said.

"Maybe, but I've still got all this stuff to learn about tuber-
culosis, meningitis, pertussis. And immunizations for travelers."

"You will. Just be patient with yourself."

"Now I know why it's called middle management," I muttered as I dodged gnarled tree roots and swerved around boulders jutting into the groomed trail. I felt tears creeping into
my throat. "I'm the one stuck in the middle. I'm not looking
forward to going back."

Jerry stopped and waited on the side of the trail for me to
catch up with him.

"I know what you mean," he said, offering me the water bottle
he'd pulled from his daypack. "I sure was ready for this break."

With ten years of experience as a classroom interpreter,
Jerry was skilled in his role as an intermediary between hearing

teachers and deaf students. He didn't mind if the teachers and hearing students ignored him; that was a sign he was doing his job well. Lately, though, he'd been feeling invisible to the administration, too.

"They don't get that if we're not there, these kids can't learn," he said.

For years, both of us had viewed our work as a way to be of service in the world. Quakers often use the term *calling* to describe such God-given, or Spirit-led tasks that demand effort and attention over a long period of time. Away from jobs, though, we wondered if we were making any difference and if the demands of our work were worth it. As the hike progressed, my questioning and complaining felt like pleas to God for guidance. Were my thoughts of moving to Stehekin an escape? Or was I sensing a nudge to seek a life more balanced between inward and outward action? If I ever did that, would I be turning my back on the injustices I felt God had called me to work on?

This year, the questions seemed to be demanding new answers. But, as on hikes in previous years, our return trek to the trailhead brought with it doubts, excuses, and declarations that our notions about living in Stehekin wouldn't work

"It's exciting to imagine moving here," I said, "but honestly, I don't think I could survive without hearing Bob Edwards' voice on *Morning Edition* each day when I wake up."

"Yeah, I know you need your daily hit of NPR," Jerry said.

"And I think it would be hard to get along without a phone and a grocery store."

"Plenty of people manage just fine doing all their business by mail," Jerry reminded me. "You've been to potlucks here and seen the spreads of food. Seems to me the locals do all right mailing their grocery lists to Safeway and getting their orders delivered on the boat. We could do that, too."

"Hmm, I guess so," I said.

We walked in quiet companionship, the kind that comes after fourteen years of marriage. Once again, hiking with Jerry in the rugged beauty of the wilderness, I felt unburdened of doubts. Just two months earlier I'd legally become Iris and embraced the prospect of blossoming into that new identity. Now, as the sound of the Agnes Gorge waterfall faded, I had new questions about who I was. The thought of moving to a place where there were no nursing jobs, an appealing possibility at the start of the hike, filled me with uncertainty by the end.

"I don't imagine the kids would want to leave their friends and all the activities at school," Jerry said, a little further down the trail. "They're not big into shopping or going to movies, but they do enjoy soccer and baseball and watching *The Cosby Show*. How would they do without team sports? And television?" And then came the biggest roadblock of all. "Besides, how would we support ourselves?"

"You're probably right," I muttered, "but it's fun to think about."

Which is just what I was doing a few days later as I drove back to Bellingham alone. In order to stretch my vacation, midway through July I returned to Bellingham for a few days of work. I boarded *The Lady* around two p.m. for the two-and-a-half- hour ride to Fields Point Landing at the lake's midpoint. The sky was clear, and the turquoise lake was flat calm. I picked up our Ford Tempo where it had sat for two weeks in the sunny parking lot at the landing. The car seats were hot, and the interior smelled like stale popcorn. I rolled down the windows, turned on the radio, and began the three-hour drive home through ranch-land, west along the winding Wenatchee

River road, over a mountain pass, and the last stretch north on the interstate to Bellingham. That July night was quiet along the deserted mountain roadway, but my mind wasn't. Part of me was dreading the deskful of communicable disease reports and the immunization clinic schedule that would fill the coming week. Another part of me was still in Stehekin in Wally's A-frame cabin with Jerry and the kids.

A couple of hours into the drive, static started to drown out the music; radio signals couldn't penetrate the ragged rock ridges approaching the ski area at Stevens Pass. In the stillness of my solitary journey, the evening air swirled in through the car window. Even without the scent of *ceanothus* to jog my memory, I re-played images of the previous two weeks.

As the Ford's diesel engine haltingly inched up toward Stevens Pass, the sun headed toward slumber, and the stars awakened. Occasional headlights appeared in my rearview mirror, probably city folks heading home after a weekend of hiking. Periodically, a semi's bright lights would blink as it headed east. My heart rate quickened and my mind raced with ideas about making Stehekin our home for at least a year. I imagined quitting my job and renting our house out. Even as I thought to myself, *this is crazy,* I felt a presence, urging me along, stripping away obstacles. It wasn't that I heard a booming, God-like voice speaking to me, but I sensed a wisdom there with me, opening me to a vision of how things could be. The energy that was compelling me seemed to be coming from a different level of awareness than my usual decision-making approach listing pros and cons, obstacles and opportunities. Another Quaker term, *leading,* conveys that awareness of being urged by God to take some action, and that night I was feeling led as surely as the highway was routing me over the mountain pass.

By the time I returned to our house in Bellingham a few hours later, I had devised a plan. Even if God was leading me, I couldn't set aside my systematic, organizational style. Before I went to bed, I filled two pages with ideas about taking a leave of absence, becoming a freelance nurse consultant, and advertising in Quaker circles for renters for our house. The next morning, I scribbled a letter to Jerry and the kids that included just three sentences about my thoughts on the drive home: *I had lots of time to fantasize about living in Stehekin. I think we should talk more about how we might swing it for seventh and eighth grade! Anyway, it helped me cover the miles and to be able to face going to work this morning.*

I put the proposal in an envelope, addressed it to Jerry Graville, General Delivery, Stehekin, WA 98852, and dropped it in the mail on my way to work; I didn't want to chance the realities of my "downlake" life eroding my dream before my return "uplake" in a week. I just hoped that when *The Lady* delivered the mail to the Stehekin landing, postmaster Don would get word to Jerry that there was a letter for him.

CHAPTER 4

Just for One Year

A WEEK LATER AS I DROVE OVER THE MOUNTAIN PASS, my focus shifted away from outbreaks and immunizations and toward my strategy for a year of escape. I schlepped my ice chest and backpack from the parking lot at Fields Point to the boat dock and wondered if my general delivery envelope had reached Jerry and the kids.

By the time *The Lady* glided up to the Stehekin landing, my heart was thumping. I tried to read my family's smiles and hugs when they met me at the boat. The kids bubbled with stories about the past week's fishing, hiking, and bakery excursions. Did this mean they'd gotten the letter and liked the idea of returning to Stehekin for a longer stay? Was Jerry's embrace a sign he wanted to hop off the treadmill, too? As we drove to

Wally's cabin, I listened to their chatter and repeatedly swallowed my questions. The minute we were inside and had unloaded the perishable groceries I'd brought with me, the words tumbled out.

"Did you get my letter?"

"We sure did," Jerry said. "Don told us he had something for us."

"It was cool to get mail at the post office," Matt chimed in.

"Well? What do you think about moving to Stehekin?"

"You still wanting to do it?" Jerry asked. He and the kids stared at me, no one taking a breath.

Was he kidding? Once I'd stuck the stamp on the envelope, excitement had throbbed all week long with the vision that was taking form. I hadn't said anything to my co-workers, not wanting to raise speculation that I might quit, but midweek, I'd confided in two long-time friends. I called Jan, a public health colleague in another city, and sketched out my thoughts about quitting my job and doing independent public health consulting. Another friend, Pat, drove the ninety miles from Seattle to Bellingham for dinner one evening and cheered my idea to take a break from full-time nursing and pursue my interests in writing, art, and music. Both women told me it would be a great adventure.

"Well, yeah," I said to Jerry, "I've been daydreaming about it all week. I've got tons of ideas about how we could do it."

Jerry looked at Rachel and Matt, and then at me. "But what about your work?"

"I'm ready for a break. What I'd really like to do is work at the bakery here. And I want to write, and read, and hike, and… just be."

I paused for a breath and looked at their grinning faces.

"When we got your letter," Jerry said, "we thought it was a great idea. But we figured you would've changed your mind by the time you got back here."

Not only had I not changed my mind, I'd grown even more committed. I felt ready to take a hard look at what I was supposed to be doing in my life, but I didn't think I had the courage to walk away from my nursing job to work in a bakery, or write, or study art in Bellingham. People might think I was irresponsible or flakey, or worse, had failed as a nurse. In Stehekin, I'd be among people who were pursuing their dreams. Like Jean, a fiber artist I'd gotten to know over the years of our vacation visits. She could have sold her wall hangings in big city galleries, but she'd opted for the solitude of the valley with her husband and son. And Tammy, who had succeeded at first-class bakeries in cities and resort towns but preferred life in the mountains with her young son and work at the smaller Stehekin Pastry Company.

No, I hadn't cooled on the plan. But, was my family really on board?

"Sounds like she's really ready for this," Jerry said to the kids. "Are you guys still up for it?"

"Yeah," Matt said, almost before Jerry finished the question.

Rachel fingered through the stack of mail I'd brought with me from Bellingham.

"But just for one year," she said.

That night, once the kids were asleep upstairs, Jerry and I stayed up late talking about what we'd need to do to make this move.

"People are going to think we're crazy," I said.

"Maybe," Jerry said. "But I bet a lot of people will wish they were doing the same thing—or something similar."

"My mom is going to freak out."

"Probably. She can't say too much, though. What we're do-ing isn't all that different from your family's move to Bellmont."

He was right about that. In 1963, the year I turned ten, my parents and I had moved from the suburbs of Chicago to a town of three hundred in Southern Illinois. The previous summer, we'd gone there on vacation to visit cousins, and my parents had been enchanted by the sound of roosters crowing at dawn and a rundown farmhouse on half an acre that was for sale. With-in a few months, my dad quit his secure job as a maintenance painter at Motorola, he and my mom sold the house they'd just finished remodeling, and we left city life behind.

Jerry put his arm around me and kissed my forehead. "Are you getting cold feet?"

"No," I sighed. "There's just a lot to do to make it work." I rummaged around the kitchen for a pencil and piece of scrap paper. "Might as well start now," I said, printing TO DO at the top of the sheet: *pay off credit card bills, cut expenses, find renters for Bellingham house, get jobs in Stehekin, find a place to live in Stehekin.*

"Why don't we start on the Stehekin things while we're still here?" Jerry said. Hunting for jobs and housing in Stehekin would be a challenge once we returned to Bellingham; Stehek-in had no daily newspaper with ads for houses to rent or job openings and no phone service to call potential employers or landlords. Maybe it was unrealistic to find work and a place to live for the following year, but we figured we should try.

First we tackled the job search. Jerry and I knew we wouldn't be able to pursue our current careers in Stehekin. There were no deaf students in the one-room school there, and the only in-terpreters in the Valley worked for the National Park Service, "interpreting" for visitors the ecology, wildlife, and history of the 684,000 acres of national park that surrounded Stehekin. Nor was there a public health department—or for that matter, any kind of health care facility—for Stehekin's residents; illnesses or injuries that couldn't be handled by one of the three EMTs who lived there were taken care of downlake. But with both of us disillusioned with our jobs and wondering if we were being led to new kinds of work, the absence of opportunities in our chosen fields made the move that much more attractive.

When we'd relocated to Seattle in 1981 for Jerry to attend an interpreter training program and for me to go to graduate school in nursing, Jerry had found part-time work as a bus driver for Seattle's public transit system, Metro. That training, experience, and commercial driver's license gave him a marketable skill that was valuable in a place like Stehekin. Although there were plenty of vehicles barged up Lake Chelan for use by long-term residents, visitors who arrived on the passenger ferry needed transportation if they wanted to venture beyond the boat landing. During our visits over the years, we'd ridden in a vintage school bus to have dinner at "The Ranch," nine miles from the landing. Run by the Courtneys, a long-time Stehekin family, the Stehekin Valley Ranch offered small tent cabins for lodging and the best flank steak, trout, blackberry pie, and cowboy coffee we'd ever tasted. Although we never stayed in the cabins, we usually treated ourselves at least once during Stehekin vacations to a bus ride and dinner at the Ranch.

This year's outing to the Ranch gave Jerry the chance to talk to Cliff Courtney about the possibility of work as a bus driver. The two chatted outside the dining room after dinner while the kids and I watched deer grazing in the pasture where the family kept their Norwegian Fjord horses used on pack trips.

On the bus ride home, Jerry told me about his conversation with Cliff.

"He said he thought he could probably use me a few days a week. He wants me to send him a letter when we get home."

"How do you think he'll be to work with?" I asked.

"He already reminded me this isn't Seattle and he doesn't have a fancy city bus."

"Well, that's sure true," I said as the aged school bus creaked along the narrow, winding gravel road.

"But, as long as we don't talk politics or religion, it'll probably be fine. Oh, and he also offered us housing for the summer."

"You're kidding."

We hadn't known that during the summer, Cliff and his family lived at the Ranch instead of in the house they were building on Company Creek Road, about five miles from the boat landing. As hard as it was to find inexpensive rentals in Stehekin in the summer, we figured we could manage at Cliff's place even if the bedrooms weren't finished and they hadn't put doors on the kitchen cabinets yet.

Cliff's offer was better than I could have imagined, and it emboldened me to talk to his sister-in-law, Robbie Courtney, about working at her Stehekin Pastry Company. The next day, I saw Robbie at the boat landing picking up a delivery of sacks of flour and sugar, flats of eggs, and crates of milk and butter.

"Robbie, can I give you a hand with this stuff?"

"Sure. Thanks."

"How's your summer been at the bakery?" I asked.

"Good," she said, flopping a fifty-pound bag of whole-wheat pastry flour into the bed of her aged pickup. "Busy."

"We've sure enjoyed coming in while we've been here this month. We've got quite a tab going."

"Yeah, I noticed when the kids got ice cream the other day that your sheet in the charge notebook is getting pretty full."

"Don't worry, we'll settle up before we leave."

"I'm not worried. I know where to find you."

We both laughed as we loaded the last items into the truck.

I hoped my attempt at humor hid my nervousness as I worked up my courage to ask Robbie for a job. When Jerry and I were first dating, we'd learned bread making from a friend, a tool and die maker who baked bread twice a week for his family of six. Faithfully following the *Tassajara Bread Book* whole-wheat bread recipe, I too made golden loaves for our household each week as well as the occasional cinnamon rolls and bagels. Stehekin could be my chance to shed my identity as a nurse and try on a new role, if Robbie would consider adding a middle-aged novice like me to her bakery crew.

"Robbie, we've been doing a lot of thinking this month, and we've decided to move here for a year starting next summer. Would you take me on as a beginning baker? I bake bread at home all the time."

"You willing to come in at four in the morning?"

"Sure," I said. "I could work full-time if you need me."

"Well, I'll have to see how the staffing comes together for next season, but I imagine I could use you. Let's stay in touch during the winter and spring."

With jobs and housing tentatively lined up, my excitement grew; I started to think this plan might actually work. We decided now was the time to look for a house to rent during the school year, too, because Cliff's offer was just for the summer season; he and his family would move back into their house after Labor Day. He suggested we talk to Mike and Nancy Barnhart. Mike, a descendant of the Courtney clan, had lived much of his life in Stehekin and had built a house on Company Creek Road, not far from Cliff's place. Like many people in Stehekin, Mike cobbled together a variety of jobs over the years so that he could pursue his passion for photography. During the summer he sold his photo prints and post cards in a small shop at the landing, and over the years we'd often chatted with him there. He and Nancy and their two sons had been living in Stehekin year-round until their oldest had graduated from eighth grade the year before and they'd moved to Wenatchee. Although they still spent the summers in Stehekin, they faced many years of dividing their time between the two places until both boys finished high school. When we asked Mike about renting their Stehekin house the following school year, he seemed as relieved as we were about the arrangement.

With just a few days left before the end of our vacation, we told the kids about our conversations with Cliff, Robbie, and the Barnharts.

"So, all we have left to do before we go back to Bellingham is talk to the teacher, Mr. Scutt, about the two of you coming here for seventh grade," Jerry told them one night as we cleaned up after dinner. "How does that sound to you?"

"Great!" Matt said. "I think it'll be fun."

"Me, too," Rachel said, plopping down on the couch. She crossed her arms across her chest, scrunching up the image of Minnie Mouse on her T-shirt. "But only for seventh grade. I want to go to Kulshan for eighth."

When we'd started our month in Stehekin, Rachel and Matt were anticipating entering sixth grade that fall at the brand new Kulshan Middle School. Rachel had brought along her new blue and white duffel bag inscribed in silver with her name and an image of the Kulshan mascot, a soaring thunderbird. All month she'd told people how she'd be in the first class at the school. Matt, more introverted than his twin sister, seemed unfazed about the coming change. Both kids, though, expressed disappointment when, mid-way through our vacation, we learned that a fire at the school's construction site had destroyed much of the building; it would not open in the fall as planned. Rachel insisted she would still use her Kulshan bag for the next year at the six-hundred-student Whatcom Middle School she and Matt would attend instead and that she would bring it with her for her seventh-grade year at the Stehekin School.

"Well, I'm only going to talk to Mr. Scutt about next year," I said. "Who knows how any of us will feel about Stehekin once we're living here instead of just on vacation?"

The next afternoon, I found Ron Scutt at the bicycle rental kiosk he and his wife operated when school was out.

"Hey, Iris, nice to see you. Have a seat."

I settled into one of the plastic lawn chairs next to a bin of bicycle helmets. Ron's lean, six-foot-four-inch frame bent over a red mountain bike suspended on a stand while he greased the chain and adjusted the brakes.

"We're planning to move to Stehekin," I blurted. "What would you think about having a couple more kids in the school next year?"

His head jerked up from his focus on the brakes. "You mean in September?"

"Not *this* September," I said. "A year from now. Rachel and Matt would be going into seventh grade then."

"Ohhhh," he said, fiddling again with the brakes. "That sounds great. We'd love to have them."

Later, replaying this conversation for Jerry, I realized my pronouncement might have been a bit of a shock for Ron. As the only teacher in a one-room elementary school, the addition of any number of new students would have a big impact. We weren't the only ones needing some time to adjust to our move to Stehekin.

Our move to Stehekin. As the once-looming obstacles with jobs, housing, and schooling for the kids started to fade, I again felt a sense of rightness about our decision. Even now I stumble over describing our plan as a leading or calling; those terms have been misused to justify war, discrimination, and irresponsible behavior. But, as with my decision to go into nursing and our moves to both Seattle and Bellingham, the only way I could understand my ease about our upcoming sojourn in Stehekin was with my belief that something outside of us was guiding this journey.

In the couple of weeks since my late-night drive over Stevens Pass, what had seemed like a crazy fantasy had rapidly become feasible—at least for one year.

CHAPTER 5

Getting Clear

Despite the signal I'd gotten that quiet night on Stevens Pass, I didn't fully trust that a wisdom outside of me was urging me to quit my job and move my family to Stehekin. Had I been elbowed by God to take time to listen deeply for a new direction? Or was it fatigue from the suffering I'd witnessed in my work that had nudged me? Was I surrendering to a source of deeper wisdom? Or giving up when faced with my own inadequacies? Although Jerry sensed, as I did, that this move was part of a larger call to re-examine the direction of our lives, he had doubts, too. We went to our Quaker meeting to help us test this desire.

A yearning for a spiritual community had spurred Jerry and me to a Quaker meeting years before. Though I'd grown up in the Lutheran church and Jerry had been brought up as a Baptist, we both had questioned those traditions as college students. In our late twenties, we had found each other, and a more relevant church home, in an intentional ecumenical community in the inner city of Evansville, Indiana. Mutual friends had started the community and introduced us, nurturing our spiritual lives, our social justice consciousness, and our relationship. In 1979, two community members, ordained United Methodist ministers, had married us in the living room of the small house our group used as its base for neighborhood ministry and worship. Two years later, Jerry and I had recognized we needed more education to pursue our respective careers and found that Seattle offered programs for both of us. By that time, I was pregnant and due in July. We'd moved in the spring in order to settle in before the birth and the start of fall classes.

Part of our settling in included hunting for a church home without the stiffness of traditional worship services and one that was involved in peace and justice work. Quaker Meeting had made our list of places to try out. At that point, our only acquaintance with Quakerism, more formally known as the Religious Society of Friends, was through the American Friends Service Committee. We'd handed out anti-war brochures from the organization a couple of years earlier in Evansville when registration for a military draft had been re-instituted. Once in Seattle, we'd made our way to the meetinghouse near the University of Washington one Sunday in April.

We paused in the doorway of the worship room, scanning the rows of molded plastic chairs arranged in a circle, before choosing two seats near the wall of floor-to-ceiling windows. Called Meeting for Worship, this hour of sitting in silence with no minister, no liturgy, no hymn-singing, no kneeling and standing, no scripture reading, and no sermons, was nothing like the Lutheran services of my youth. Neither did it much resemble the house church we'd attended in Evansville, with folk songs accompanied by a guitar and communion with homemade whole wheat bread and a common cup of wine. At first I fidgeted, wondering when someone would say something. Eventually I closed my eyes, focused on my breath, and blocked out the sounds of crows skittering across the skylight and the whoosh of bus doors opening and closing at the Metro stop on the corner. I found comfort in the quiet presence of a hundred others doing the same.

Jerry and I talked later about how we both had felt at home in that simple space and service. Over the coming months, we attended regularly and were welcomed by other couples having babies, as well as seniors and singles who, when our baby unexpectedly turned out to be twins, became surrogate aunts, uncles, and grandparents. We came to recognize that Quakerism was our path. For me, it was a place that not only allowed, but encouraged, my questions about God and faith. It affirmed my belief that my faith, my work, and the way I live my life are all of the same cloth, and it gave me tools and a vocabulary, such as the terms *leading* and *calling*, to open to a source of love and wisdom outside of myself to discern what I'm meant to do with my life.

Early Quakers like George Fox and William Penn confessed their own tendencies, so familiar to me, to be guided by fear, power, and self-importance. Their mystical encounters with God emboldened them to oppose religious, political, social, financial, and legal systems that advocated violence and inequality. Quaker John Woolman's seeking led him to oppose slavery; Lucretia Mott joined Woolman's abolition work and, with Susan B. Anthony, spoke out for women's rights.

The Clearness Committee is one process Friends have developed to help people discern when, or even if, the Spirit is leading them. It's like going to your favorite aunt when you're trying to make a decision. She nods slightly as you weigh pros and cons; she responds to your wonderings with gentle questions that unlock the answers inside you.

One squally fall evening, four Quaker "aunts and uncles" joined Jerry and me in our living room. Wind off Bellingham Bay blew rain sideways across the picture window. One of the Clearness Committee members, Sue, served as facilitator. After about fifteen minutes of sinking into the silence, just as we do in Quaker worship, she explained that the committee's purpose was to support us in listening for inward guidance, not to tell us what to do. She then asked us to explain the decision we were seeking clarity about. Jerry and I took turns describing our plan to quit our jobs, rent our house in Bellingham, and spend a year in Stehekin.

"We feel like we're moving too fast and spending too much time working to support a lifestyle that doesn't nourish us," Jerry said.

"For over twenty years, I've been passionate about nursing," I said. "I've approached public health with fervor, believing this was the work I was meant to do. Over the last couple of years, though, I've felt frustrated and discouraged." I took a deep breath. "I don't like being angry with my clients when they make choices that aren't good for themselves and their children."

I felt embarrassed by my admission, but, once asked, I couldn't hold back my words or my tears. "And I'm so tired of the bureaucracy surrounding public health decisions. It seems it's all about money and not what's best for people. This isn't how I want to feel about my work."

I looked around the circle at Jerry and our friends. Some of them nodded, others had their eyes closed but were listening intently. Sue cleared her throat.

"What kinds of sacrifices would you have to make to do this?" she asked.

Sue's question hung in the air as I mentally clicked off what I'd "give up" by moving to Stehekin: television, shopping malls, telephones, a grocery store a mile away open twenty-four hours a day. Those were the losses people often cited when we talked about life in Stehekin, but I welcomed being free of their intrusions. As the committee waited, I thought to myself that to not follow through with the plan would have felt like a sacrifice. But that wasn't the full answer. The silence stretched out, my heart quickened, and I swallowed hard around the lump in my throat. I took a deep breath and puffed air through my lips.

"I'd have to sacrifice my identity as a nurse," I finally answered. "That's how I've presented myself to the world for over twenty years. I've never struggled to describe who I am as long as I've had that title."

I had assumed I would work as a nurse all of my life, in fact, that I was a nurse to my very core. When peers talked about living for their days off when they could do what they really loved, I felt deep gratitude that I'd been led to a career that was so much more than a job to me. I treasured the ways it sated my curiosity about anatomy, physiology, and pathophysiology at the same time it offered an outlet for my compassion for others. My work and my desire to serve had coalesced. Now, without that, who would I be?

"What is it about moving to Stehekin that will help you discover if you're called to other work?" someone on our Clearness Committee asked.

I could answer this question without hesitation. "There's no option of nursing work there, so people won't see me as a nurse and won't have expectations that I'll keep climbing the professional ladder with more and more leadership and responsibility. And although I know I can hear God anywhere, I need the slower pace and solitude to listen."

That night, the Clearness Committee's questions helped me answer some of my own. I suspected more uncertainty would arise for both Jerry and me throughout our year of preparation, but I knew that this group would be there to listen again.

CHAPTER 6

Not Courage–Rightness

With jobs and housing lined up in Stehekin and the support of our Quaker Clearness Committee, it was time to go public with our plan. Familiar fears resurfaced, this time projected onto others, especially my mom and co-workers; I anticipated criticism of our abandoning Middle America for the wilderness and of my leaving a successful, secure career in public health. I didn't want the people we cared about to hear our news first from someone else, so we started with the easiest ones, Jerry's parents.

Windsor and Florence both had been born and raised in Junction City, Oregon, about fifteen miles from the university town of Eugene. They still lived in the house they bought as newlyweds in 1947. From the time Rachel and Matt were a year old, Jerry's folks had hosted them for a week in Junction City every summer so Jerry and I could have some time alone. That summer of 1993, though, all four of us headed to Junction City soon after our month in Stehekin. The first day, Florence and I stocked the fridge for the week while the kids played in the backyard and Jerry and his dad poked around in Windsor's shop. Windsor's collection of rusty farm equipment, boxes of used auto parts, and countless other cast-offs had earned him the nickname, "The Gadget King." Over dinner that night, we learned he and Jerry had unearthed a 1952 mint-green GMC pickup.

"It was my dad's truck," Windsor said.

"Grampa Arthur built a wooden canopy over the bed, wired it, and used it for camping and hunting trips," Jerry said.

"Does it still run?" I asked.

"Don't know for sure," Windsor said. "It's been sitting in the shop for about twenty years. But it's got a pretty simple engine. I think I could probably get it going again."

"Then what would you do with it?" Florence asked.

"Give it to Jerry," Windsor said, slapping Jerry on the back.

Jerry looked at me, took a breath, and got up to sit down next to his mom. "We've decided we're going to live in Stehekin for a year starting next summer, and I think this would be a great Stehekin rig."

Florence's chin trembled as she twisted her fingers in her lap.

"I think living in Stehekin sounds like a grand adventure," Windsor said. "Florence, remember how much we enjoyed that time a couple of summers ago when we met up with them after the kids had been here visiting us?"

"Yes, I do," Florence said, dabbing her teary eyes with the Kleenex she always seemed to have tucked in a shirt cuff or pocket. "It's a special place, but awfully remote, isn't it?"

"You could come visit us, Gramma," Matt said.

"And we'll write you letters," Rachel added. Don't worry, Gramma, we'll be OK."

"You guys are always doing something interesting," she said. "Interesting" was her catch-all word for anything she didn't fully understand. "I'm sure this will be a great experience. And Arthur's truck probably will like being in Stehekin, too."

Over the next week, Jerry and his dad worked all day and into the night cleaning and replacing truck parts. Periodically, one of them would try turning the engine over, and we'd hear the old rig choke, sputter, and die. The day before we were scheduled to return to Bellingham, Florence, the kids, and I heard a whoop from the driveway. We rushed outside to see a grinning, grease-covered father and son leaning against the purring truck.

"Jerry decided to name it 'Sir Arthur' in honor of my dad," Windsor said, adjusting the baseball cap that covered his bald head. "I think he'd approve."

The six-hour drive back to Bellingham the next day gave us time to reflect on Jerry's parents' reaction to our plan. As usual, they kept to themselves any concern they felt about us moving to a place so cut off from them. Instead, they offered support and encouragement. It was this trust that I so valued—and that I knew I wouldn't hear from my mom.

Well into my teens, I had thought my mom knew best—about clothes, friends, homework, values, and beliefs. We had clung to each other when my father, an alcoholic, died a few months after my second birthday; Mom was twenty-eight. Whatever my two-year-old reasoning made of losing my father, I likely believed that if only I was "good enough," I could spare my mom more pain and protect us both from more loss.

Mom married Chuck when I was five, and I immediately called him "Dad." His steadfast love must have eased some of the self-blame young children often bear after a parent's death. Once, after I'd started school, I came home to find a handwritten rhyming poem he'd left for me; it ended, "All in all you're quite a girl/I bless the day I met your mother, Shirl."

Dad guided my growing up without Mom's overlay of caution. As I moved into adulthood and started to form my own opinions, he seemed to understand the deep wounds Mom carried from an alcoholic father and first husband as well as her terror that she would lose me as well. "Be careful," was always her farewell, accompanied by tears and long hugs when I left the house and also when I returned.

One of our last times to travel together as a family was the three-hundred-mile drive home to Southern Illinois after my cousin's wedding in Chicago. We started the journey late at night after the wedding reception; the next day, I'd leave for nursing school in Evansville, Indiana, fifty miles away from home. I was in the backseat of our blue Pontiac Bonneville, Dad driving and Mom in the passenger seat, chain-smoking Pall Malls.

"That was a fun wedding," I said.

"Fun for everybody else, but lots of work for Auntie Ann," my mom said, her cigarette glowing in the dark. "At least she doesn't have to worry any more about Pam bringing home some black guy or getting pregnant before she's married."

I looked straight ahead at the oncoming cars on Highway 41, debating about whether to challenge my mom's judgment about this older cousin I admired. I stayed quiet and watched Mom lean over to look at the dashboard.

"Chuck, slow down a bit. I know we've got a long drive ahead of us, but I want to get there in one piece." Mom took a long drag on her cigarette and blew the smoke out into the small sliver of air where she'd rolled down the passenger window. "I have a feeling Barbara's going to be a handful for Auntie Ann for awhile still. She'll probably make her older sister look like an angel."

"Now, Shirl, you're being pretty tough on those girls," Dad said, not taking his eyes off the highway. "That's all part of growing up." In the glow of the car's control panel, I could see his hands tighten on the steering wheel.

"You mean causing your mother sleepless nights and giving her gray hair? You think that's what kids are supposed to do?"

"Well, we've been pretty lucky with our punkin,'" he said, glancing at me in the rearview mirror. "She hasn't caused us much worry."

"Thanks, Dad," I said, scrunching down into the seat.

"Now, don't start crying," Mom said. "I can hear you sniffling. But your dad's right. At least you haven't been sleeping around the way Julie and Cathy have. Or gotten into smoking or drugs."

I saw a little smile tug at the corner of Dad's mouth. "Honey, you're one to talk about smoking," he said. "How many cigarettes have you had since we've gotten in the car?"

"Do as I say, not as I do. Besides, this is a stressful day." A halo of smoke hovered over her head, casting a gray glow on her short, brown hair.

I closed my eyes and braced for another of her rants. I was eighteen, but felt like I was three.

"Who knows what you'd be like if I hadn't kept such a close eye on you? I think Julie and Cathy's moms didn't know what they were doing half the time. And I bet their parents wouldn't spend seven hours in the car making sure they get to college on time after a family wedding the way we are."

"I appreciate you doing this," I said.

"Well, it's just what I've done all my life. That's what being a parent is all about—making sacrifices for your child. And I've made plenty of them." She undid the clasp of her leather cigarette case, slid another Pall Mall into her mouth, and sucked in as the glow of her lighter brightened her face. "All those years when I worked all day and then did other people's ironing at night so I could keep a roof over our heads and food on the table, not to mention pay for your tap and ballet lessons. And then after Chuck and I got married, we both worked hard to do the kinds of things our parents never could, like take vacations to Florida and Québec. I'm sorry I've made you cry, but this is the truth. Do you know how many years I wore the same dresses to work so you could have new clothes for school? Did you think those skirts and sweaters from Wood's Department Store grew on trees?"

"Honey, take it easy," my dad interrupted. "This is our last night together before she leaves for school."

"No, I won't go easy, she needs to hear this." Mom twisted around to face me. After the long day at the wedding and the reception, her red lipstick was a blur and her mascara a smudge under her eyes. "Sometimes you can be pretty selfish, you know, just concerned about me, me, me. There are lots of kids out there who have it way worse than you and are damn grateful for everything they get. I just hope someday you'll realize how lucky you are. This is what loving someone more than life itself is all about."

"I'm sorry, Mom," I whispered around the tears clogging my throat. "I'm really grateful for everything you've done for me. I know you've worked hard so I could have it easier than you did." My indebtedness was genuine. It would take dozens of hours of therapy for me to hear this attack—as well as lesser ones she'd delivered in my teens and twenties—without questioning my worth. And in another thirty years, as I sent my own children off to college, I'd understand my mom's grief at my leaving.

"Well, I didn't want our last evening to turn into a lecture," she said after a long inhale on her cigarette. "I just hope you never have to go through some of the things I did, because I'm not sure you'd survive."

Highway lights brightened the dark car enough for me to see Dad's head shaking slightly, his eyes in the rearview mirror, searching for mine.

*   *   *

MOM ALWAYS IMAGINED THE WORST WHENEVER someone was sick. The night five years later when she called about Dad's loss of energy, I thought she was overly concerned. By then he was fifty-four and a self-employed house painter, working long hours standing, scraping peeling paint and wallpaper, and hoisting extension ladders and heavy drop cloths. No wonder he always headed for his recliner after dinner. That's where I found him the next night when I arrived from Evansville, where I was teaching at my nursing school alma mater. I bent to kiss his cheek.

His right hand trembled as he touched the spot I'd just kissed. "Huh? Oh, hi." He looked at me blankly, then shifted his gaze to the dark TV screen across the room.

"I'm glad to see you, Dad. How are you doing?"

"Okay." Both hands trembled as he pressed them into the arms of his chair and squirmed in the seat. He did a little shuffle with his feet on the carpet as if he was trying to get traction on a slippery floor. "Do you want some lunch?"

I swallowed hard. "No, that's okay, I already ate."

Mom hadn't been exaggerating. Dad needed to see a doctor. Baffled by what he saw, the family doctor referred Dad to Dr. Chen, a neurologist. After weeks of blood tests to rule out heavy metal poisoning from paint, or exposure to a toxin while serving in the Marines in Korea, Dr. Chen diagnosed a degenerative neurological condition.

"I think it's Creutzfeld-Jakob Disease," Dr. Chen told Mom and me in the hallway outside the exam room. "Can't know for sure except at autopsy. Can do nothing here."

"Nothing?" my mom asked. Her voice and her lips trembled.

My mind rolodexed through stacks of note cards I had written in nursing school, a technique to remember all the diseases that can destroy the complex transmission of signals from the brain to the rest of the body. I retrieved just enough to believe that what Dr. Chen told us was true. Now, medicine knows about what is commonly referred to as Mad Cow Disease, but back in 1976, it was a mystery. All I could do was put my arm around my mom's shoulders and blink away my own tears.

"Well, we could send him to the National Institutes of Health..." Dr. Chen said.

"In Bethesda, Maryland?"

My question was a stall for time to think. I knew he was referring to the research center, a thousand miles from my parents' southern Illinois home. I had completed a six-week independent nursing study on the cancer unit there just the year before. In the early days of that term, I had fantasized that cures for cancer were incubating in laboratories down the hall. That dream faded as I cared for people going through drug trials to test what dose would cause intolerable side effects. I monitored their vomiting, hair loss, and confusion, knowing that none of the medications offered a promise of cure. I stood at a woman's bedside as she was sedated while doctors raised her body temperature to 107°F attempting, literally, to fry ovarian cancer cells. And I watched a man in his mid-twenties like me, sign consent form after consent form, hoping that the never-ending experiments would lead to his miracle cure. He died just before I left.

Now this place was being offered as the only option for treatment for my dad.

As I drove my parents from the doctor's office toward their home, the city landscape blurred into farm implement stores and plowed fields. My dad trembled and dozed in the backseat while my mom silently held his hand. A debate raged in my mind.

"I can't do it, Mom," I said later that night, sitting across from her at her kitchen table. "I can't send him there." I could barely talk around the ache radiating from my heart to my throat. "I saw people die there, all alone and in pain. That's not what I want, and I don't think it's what he would want, either."

I expected her to argue with me, to insist that we not give up, that we try everything possible. Those were the justifications I'd come up with in the car as I considered Dr. Chen's suggestion. Dad had always been there for me, shouldn't I agree to any—likely the only—action that might save him?

My mom, her eyes red-rimmed from an afternoon and evening of crying, stared silently into her cup of Lipton's tea and nodded. For once, she wasn't criticizing; for once, not challenging my opinion.

We kept Dad at home where he could sit in his TV chair, watching, but not comprehending, that his beloved Chicago Bears were losing yet again. He could eat my mom's meatloaf and eight-layer salad. Could sip his black coffee, until he couldn't any more. Soon he didn't know where he was, couldn't stand up or walk without a supportive arm around him, and hugged me too intimately, thinking I was his wife.

A few months later when a phlegmy cough rattled in Dad's chest and created the perfect environment for pneumonia, he went into the hospital across town from the one where I taught. Dr. Chen was there, again, with nothing to offer.

When oxygen couldn't get into Dad's swollen airways, he went into a coma. I had learned in nursing school that hearing is the last sense to fade, so I kept talking to him, even though he couldn't speak. One afternoon when Mom took a break from Dad's bedside, I stroked the silver hair at his temples and swabbed his dry lips.

"Thank you Dad," I whispered. "You did your job well. I'll be okay."

A few days later, he took his last, labored breath. He had been my defender when my mom demanded perfection. He had provided unconditional love. In standing up for me, he had taught me to stand up for myself. And for him.

It might have been easier for my mom if my standing up for myself had come years earlier with my dad still beside her as I stepped out independently. Or later, when his death was not so raw for her. But I couldn't defer the journey I needed to take any more than a toddler could postpone learning to walk.

Within months after Dad died, Mom had moved to Evansville, to the same apartment complex where I lived. I had become more involved with the intentional community

I worshipped with in the inner city and had started to offer blood pressure clinics in the neighborhood. When I rented an apartment there, Mom scoffed at my desire to live among the people I was serving. She was convinced the community was brainwashing me. A month after my move, Jerry arrived from San Francisco to get involved in the community's work, and our romance blossomed.

I postponed introducing Jerry to my mom until I knew our relationship was solid. She always volunteered her snap judgments whenever she met guys I was dating: "Nice, but not very exciting;" or "Charming, but I don't trust him;" and her favorite, "I sure don't know what you see in him." When she finally joined Jerry and me for a vegetarian dinner at my aging apartment, disapproval lined her face. Months later, my throat felt coated with cotton when I called to ask if we could stop by her place one Sunday afternoon.

After she directed Jerry and me to the couch in her living room, words tumbled from my mouth. "We're getting married on September 22nd," I said, "at the house in our neighborhood where we attend worship." A quick swallow. "I hope you and Gram will come."

Her eyes narrowed. "I don't know," she said, looking only at me as if Jerry wasn't there. "I don't understand this so-called community you're part of, and I don't support what you're doing." She shifted in her chair toward the patio door so that I saw more of her back than her face. Red blotches crept up her neck, and her jaw clenched. "I'd feel like a hypocrite to be a part of something I don't approve of."

"I'm sorry you feel that way," Jerry said as he reached for my hand and held it firmly. "We'd like you to be there."

"I'll have to think about it," she said, still facing the door.

I wasn't sure whether to wish for her to come or to stay away.

She and my grandmother did show up at the wedding, escorted by a long-time family friend who was an attorney. I suspected she had brought him to make sure that the ceremony was legal. It was, complete with two ordained United Methodist ministers.

Over the coming years, my mom offered only questions and criticism of our ventures. She didn't visit when Rachel and Matt, her only grandchildren, were born. By the time they were two, she and her partner, Steve, lived in Hollywood, Florida, and we all flew across the country to celebrate her birthday. Rachel dashed from the airplane into the arms of the grandmother she had never met and melted some of the iceberg between my mom and me. Despite all the ways Mom felt I'd disappointed her since I'd grown into adulthood, she could embrace these two cherubs who accepted her unconditionally.

*   *   *

WEEKS BEFORE I TOLD MOM we'd be moving to Stehekin, I muted my fretting with the fantasy that she'd see our adventure as reminiscent of the move that she, Dad, and I had made from Chicago to Bellmont, a tiny town in Southern Illinois. Nobody used the expression "mid-life crisis" then, but now, at almost the exact same stage in my life that my parents had been in theirs, I suspected they had longed for new direction just as I did. What had their colleagues thought when they both quit successful jobs, sold the house they had just remodeled, and bought a dilapidated farmhouse? Did their urban friends understand my dad's desire to wake up hearing roosters crowing and to start his own business as a painter and decorator? Could they imagine my mom, who loved to entertain and go to the theater, being happy in a town of three hundred with party lines for phone service? It turned out those years in Bellmont had been some of her happiest.

I hoped my mom was remembering those times as I told her we'd secured housing and work in Stehekin, and that the kids were looking forward to the one-room school they would attend. "And I hope you and Steve will come visit us there," I said.

"Maybe we will," she said, sounding no more certain than when she'd waffled about coming to our wedding.

*   *   *

My co-workers' reaction to my resignation was supportive—and surprising. Several of them had joined me in winter breaks in Stehekin and could understand well the allure of the mountains and the absence of public health stresses. They'd hiked with me beneath towering pines glistening with frost and laid the first tracks with our cross-country skis in fresh snow right outside the cabin door. Perhaps it was those memories that I stirred for my colleagues when I announced at a staff meeting that Jerry, the kids, and I would be going to Stehekin for a full year.

"Are you taking a leave of absence?" Peggy asked after the meeting. She whispered her question as if I were planning a prison escape.

"No, I'm resigning."

"Really?" Her voice raised an octave. "What if there aren't any openings when you come back?"

"I'm going to take a hard look at my work and what I want to do with my life," I said. "I don't know where that might lead me, and I don't want to feel obligated to come back to this job."

"Good for you," she said. "I don't think I could do that, but I admire your courage…"

Courage? I'd never considered that. More like desperation.

"I hope you'll write to us while you're gone and tell us what you're discovering."

"Ah, yes, writing is one of the things I want to do while I'm there," I said, "and I'm sure you'll be getting letters. Remember, there aren't any telephones in Stehekin."

The encouragement, and even admiration, of friends and family muzzled my mom's hesitations. The image of "Sir Arthur" resurrected for another journey heartened me. Now, many months after that late night drive over Stevens Pass when I'd felt God nudging me—us—toward this change, our decision reverberated with rightness.

CHAPTER 7

Getting Stehekinized

In January, we received some unexpected affirmation of our leap of faith. Jerry was offered a temporary, full-time job as a vocational rehabilitation counselor with a significant raise over his public school sign language interpreting position. The extra income of this new post would help us pay off credit cards and squirrel away cash for the winter months in Stehekin when we'd have no work.

Although none of us were big consumers, like many middle class American families, we usually spent what we earned. With Stehekin as our goal, we found new skill at cutting expenses and saving money. When any of us felt the pinch of belt-tightening, a single word—Stehekin—eased it. We evaluated each expenditure, from take-out pizza to movie tickets, in terms of what it would mean for our sojourn in the mountains. One night when the waitress brought our bill after dinner at a neighborhood Chinese restaurant, Rachel calculated how many cinnamon rolls and scones that would buy at the Stehekin bakery. The restaurant lost four regular customers.

"You know, what we spend every month on cable would buy us a round-trip boat ticket," Jerry said a couple of weeks later. That ended our subscription.

Over the winter, Jerry's dad continued to fine-tune Grandpa Arthur's truck; it was in top form in the spring when Jerry drove it to Bellingham, and we packed its covered bed with belongings. We also rented a cargo van and filled it to within inches of its roof with cross-country skis, bicycles, and boxes bulging with books, blank journals, games, clothes for all seasons, our Kitchen Aid mixer and mini-espresso machine, a TV and VCR to watch episodes of the television drama *E.R.* that Jerry's mom offered to record, and an Apple computer friends passed on to us when they upgraded. To ease my withdrawal from National Public Radio, a tape deck for the cassette recordings a friend would make of Bob Edwards' *Morning Edition* went in, too. I wondered if we really needed all of this for our year in the wilderness. Or would it be enough?

One weekend early in May, we drove both vehicles to Tom Courtney's barge dock in Chelan. With no roads beyond Fields Point, Tom's barge was the only way to get Sir Arthur and our boxes to their new home; we left them there for his next run to Stehekin.

After school was out in June, the four of us and our golden retriever, Murphy, squeezed into our red Ford Tempo for the final leg of our move. We left Matt and Murphy in Chelan to make the trip uplake later in the day in a four-passenger floatplane; *The Lady of the Lake* prohibited dogs during the summer season. Jerry, Rachel, and I went on to the Fields Point Landing, bought an annual pass to park the Ford there, and boarded *The Lady*.

Two-and-a-half hours later, Captain Wilsey maneuvered the boat's white body trimmed in crisp blue to the dock, her starboard side gently tapping the pilings. I slid a sweaty palm into Jerry's right hand, my pulse throbbing against his wrist; I draped my other arm over Rachel's shoulder. My heart could have been racing with worry, but this time, excitement, rather than fear, sped its beat.

The Lady's aluminum gangplank squeaked and creaked into place, bridging the boat deck to the landing. Along with other passengers, we tromped across its grated metal in waffle-soled hiking boots. The rest of the crew tossed freight from the stern; backpacks, canvas mail sacks, hard plastic ice chests, cardboard boxes—bits of the world from the other end of fifty-five-mile-long Lake Chelan seeping into this Cascade Mountains valley. Wally Winkel leaned against the landing's massive cedar sign with its carved greeting, "Welcome to Stehekin." He nodded his own welcome, and I wondered how long it would take for him to think of us as Stehekinites instead of just "tourists from the West Side."

The early June breeze lifted the sappy, earthy scent of Douglas fir, sage, and ponderosa pine. We trooped up the hill at the landing to the McGregor Mountain Outdoor Supply shop to announce our arrival to Caity Karapostoles, the store's owner. We'd met Caity and her family on our first visit to Stehekin, and their three kids and our two enjoyed playing together. Soon, like Caity and everyone else in Stehekin, we'd be mailing our grocery list to one of the stores in Chelan and picking up our order at the landing.

And we'd be making regular trips to the post office. That day, we climbed its wooden steps to the covered porch barely big enough to hold the three of us. We'd stopped here many times over the decade of our visits to check the bulletin board covering an entire wall. The post office was the communication center for the community. Thumb tacks or duct tape secured hand-made fliers about potlucks and softball games, news from people who had moved away, and official notices from the National Park Service about trail conditions. The kids especially enjoyed flipping through the clipboard of FBI "Wanted" posters by the door.

As we'd disembarked, we'd seen the postmaster, Don Pitts, loading lumpy, gray canvas sacks into a wooden cart; now empty, it rested at the end of the porch. Jerry opened the screen door, and Rachel and I squeezed into the front room of the building. We nodded to a few familiar faces as people milled around waiting for Don to open the top half of the Dutch door to his office, the signal that all of the mail had been sorted and deposited in the boxes. I stepped up to ask if he'd received our check for mailbox rental.

"Sure did," he said. "Yours is number twenty-six. Here's the combination."

I could see an envelope through the tiny glass window below the combination dial on the box's door. I remembered doing the same spin of the dial as a ten-year old in Bellmont, a transplanted city girl sent alone on an errand to get mail from the little town's post office. Soon my kids would be doing their own version of this chore on the days the mail arrived in Stehekin. The lock clicked open, and I retrieved a cellophane envelope. Inside, a postal box rental receipt for $11.25 for a year, and a handwritten note from Don. Jerry peered over my shoulder as I read: *Hi! Welcome to Stehekin! Hope your expectations will be rewarding and pleasurable. Good school, good Valley, good people. You'll fit right in.*

I sighed deeply as I slid the note back into the envelope and into my jeans pocket. Fitting in here was something I worried about. The post office bulletin board offered as many diverse viewpoints as a newspaper's op-ed pages, and I was far from agreement with many of them. I wondered if Don would still think we belonged in Stehekin once he started sorting our mail. Our magazines, newsletters, and countless return addresses would give away our liberal politics and our Quaker beliefs, values I suspected would clash with Don's reputation as an outspoken conservative and an evangelical Christian. Here, I couldn't surround myself only with people who looked at the world as I did.

I turned to the postmaster and waved.

"Thanks, Don. See you next week."

I wasn't a local yet, but Don's note in my pocket gave me hope.

Down the road from the post office we found our boxes, stacked and shrink-wrapped on four pallets at the unloading area for Tom's barge. "Sir Arthur" was parked there, too, with the key in the ignition. The old truck started up without a cough or a shudder. It fit in well with Stehekin's other vintage vehicles, right down to its expired Oregon license plates.

After the floatplane delivered Matt and Murphy, we all set off toward Cliff's house, waving to every car and truck we passed. We'd learned this bit of Stehekin etiquette on our very first visit. The other drivers knew the rule; they all waved back. Some lifted only the index finger off the steering wheel, some raised one hand, others wiggled several fingers or gave a thumbs-up. The valley opened before us—Purple Point, Rainbow Falls, Buckner Orchard. In the distance, Horseshoe Basin, Agnes Gorge, Sahale Glacier, and McGregor Mountain beckoned.

Near Harlequin Bridge, the fifty-year-old truss bridge spanning the Stehekin River, we passed Maria, a woman we knew who worked on the Park Service trail crew. We could barely see her head over the steering wheel of her Volvo station wagon. Within a few days, we discovered that Maria's vigorous, two-handed wave and her flash of a smile were standard every single time she passed someone.

We used the couple of weeks before Jerry and I started our new jobs to settle in to the Stehekin way of life. Grocery shopping, just the first of many changes to our usual routines, began at the kitchen table. There, I'd write my list, put it along with a blank check into an envelope addressed to the Safeway Store in Chelan, and get it into the outgoing mail basket at the post office before boat time. Then I'd wait for three or four days for the boxes of food to arrive on *The Lady*.

This was nothing like grocery shopping in Bellingham. There, I'd squeeze shopping in as I drove past Ennen's Market on my way to work or on my return home at the end of the day—or both. Clutching my list scrawled on the back of a used envelope—½ *gallon of milk, baking powder, broccoli, soy sauce, OJ*—I'd head for the produce section, picking through bundles of broccoli for the firmest stalks and bluest-green flower buds.

Now, I trusted a stranger named Alice to be my eyes, nose, and fingertips, hoping she'd bypass rubbery carrots and rusty lettuce leaves when she picked out my vegetables. Or that she'd avoid onions with mushy spots and pick avocados with the right amount of softness to mash them into guacamole.

Alice had been filling Stehekinites' orders for ten years. By the third time she packed up mine, I realized she shopped as if she were buying for herself. She often jotted notes on the receipt that came with our grocery boxes. Once she wrote: *The Romaine heads are really small this week and since they were 3 for $1.50, I went ahead and sent you 2 more than you ordered. Hope that was OK.* Another time she apologized: *All the bananas in stock today were over-ripe. I couldn't find a bunch I thought would survive the trip uplake. Sorry—maybe next order.*

I got more efficient preparing my grocery list once Caity gave me a map of the Safeway store and advised me to organize my order by aisles corresponding to the supermarket's floor plan. She said the system made it easier for Alice and cut down on surprises. One day as I helped Rene Courtney heap grocery boxes into her van, she told me of the time her order for a box of red vines, the licorice candy her daughter liked, turned into delivery of a box of red wine. Rene didn't seem too disappointed, but if she'd listed the request in the candy aisle, her daughter might have been happier.

Shopping for milk called for new strategies, too. In Bellingham, I'd buy a half-gallon carton every few days. Here, with two pre-adolescents and a couple of latte-guzzling adults, I'd order four, one-gallon plastic jugs at a time, then put them in the freezer. Every few days I'd have to remember to transfer one to the refrigerator for a slow thaw so it would be drinkable when we finished off the previous gallon.

The day one box load of our order didn't make it on the boat, I considered that the intrigue of this routine might fade. Maybe I'd tire of Alice's decisions when I forgot to give her precise instructions about which item to buy. Perhaps I'd long to inspect asparagus for the most-tender spears, might want to thump a cantaloupe and smell its sweetness, or take advantage of an in-store special. Then I thought of the warehouse aisles at the neighborhood store in Bellingham. Everywhere I turned there were decisions to make—smooth or crunchy; enriched, fortified, or plain; traditional or new and improved. I had to choose among five brands, three sizes, and four colors of tissue (plus scented, unscented or moisturizing), and select among the half dozen varieties of mayonnaise and three types of stone-ground mustard. For now, mail order grocery shopping and letting Alice decide for me was a relief.

Sir Arthur served us well, too, transporting freight and visitors the four miles from the boat landing to the house. One night, after an opening at the art gallery at the Visitor's Center, Jerry got behind the wheel, and the kids and I squeezed onto the cab's brown leather bench seat. It was still a bit daring for the kids to ride in a vehicle without seat belts, though the maximum speed of twenty-five on the Stehekin Valley Road made the risk of injury unlikely.

The moon's light shimmered on the lake and stars salted the black sky. Two circles of yellow from Sir Arthur's headlights were all that brightened a few feet of road ahead of us. Just past the Bakery, the lights dimmed and then disappeared.

"Dad, what happened?" Rachel said, her voice as tense as her grip on my thigh. I peered into the darkness, imagining, as I suspected Rachel was, a black bear bolting out of the trees.

"Don't know," Jerry said, slowing the truck and edging toward the road's shoulder. "Get the flashlight out of the glove box, would you, Matt?"

Jerry rolled down the window and shined the flashlight's beam toward the road as he inched the truck forward.

"Dad, you're not going to drive..." Rachel started to chide when the headlights lit up the road again.

"Yes!" Matt cheered.

Rachel loosened her hold on my leg.

As we approached Harlequin Bridge and the turn-off to the gravel road to our place, the road went black again.

"Dad!" was all Rachel got out this time.

"It's okay," Matt said, "Dad's got the flashlight. And we're almost home."

We crept beside the Stehekin River on Company Creek Road, the lights flickering on and off for the last half mile of our trip.

"We've got to get those lights fixed," Rachel said as we followed the flashlight's beam into the house. "It's too scary driving in the dark like that."

The next day, Jerry flagged down Tom Langley when their trucks met on the road, and he agreed to look at Sir Arthur after work. Tom, Maria's partner, had a reputation in the Valley for being able to fix anything electrical, having worked with the Park Service maintenance crew for years. He isolated a loose connection in the truck's forty-year-old wiring and repaired it with a bit of electrical tape and, for good measure, a little duct tape.

"Now your truck's been Stehekinized," he said.

Although Sir Arthur had made the transition, I knew it would take more than duct tape for me to feel I really belonged here. Like many small towns, the newcomer label took decades to shake in Stehekin, and people knew we'd likely move on in a year or two. Still, this valley carried a sense of home for me, and I hoped that my job at the bakery, Jerry's work at the Ranch, and the kids' enrollment in the school would strengthen our connection the way Tom's wiring job had restored the truck's lights.

With Tom's help, we kept our vintage truck running throughout the summer. As we thought ahead to winter, though, we wondered how it would hold up in the cold, snow, and ice. A possible solution appeared one day at the post office. A flier on Public Utility District letterhead pinned to the bulletin board announced that the PUD was accepting sealed bids for the purchase of its 1973 Chevrolet Suburban. We knew the car well because our neighbor, Karl Fellows, drove the faded yellow rig in his job for the PUD. Jerry learned from Karl that the utility district planned to upgrade his vehicle and needed to unload the old one; a buyer in Stehekin would be ideal.

At the end of July, Jerry mailed off his bid for $581.00. A few days later, he came home, waving an envelope with the return address "Public Utility District No. 1 of Chelan County." The letter inside informed him his offer on the vehicle had been accepted and that Karl would turn it over to us. By the next week, "Colonel Mustard" sat in our driveway, bringing us another step closer toward being Stehekinized.

CHAPTER 8

Eat Dessert First

Its official name is Stehekin Pastry Company, but everyone in the valley refers to it as, simply, "the bakery." A framed quote greets all who enter there—"Eat dessert first; life is uncertain." The bakery's glass case, filled with cinnamon rolls, breads, muffins, cookies, and pies, serves as the exclamation point for that command.

The promise of employment at the bakery had eased some of my worries about the financial risks of our move. Stepping into a baker's shoes meant more than income, though. Working in any bakery, and especially the one in Stehekin, was a long-time dream I'd carried through many of the twenty years of my public health nursing career. But until the move to Stehekin, I had thought my interests in food, art, writing, and music would have to wait until later. Besides, even though I made bread, cookies, and scones at home, I knew nothing about commercial baking, and the bakery's owner, Robbie Courtney, had a reputation as a perfectionist. Thankfully, she took a chance on me.

The afternoon before my first day on the job, I stopped into the bakery as a customer. Robbie's right-hand baker, Tammy, confirmed my start time of four a.m.

"See you tomorrow, dark and early," she said as I left, clutching a paper bag filled with black bottom cupcakes. I thought of myself as a morning person and was accustomed to nursing jobs that started at seven or eight a.m., but I was a little intimidated by the requirement to arrive at work before dawn. The early part was one adjustment; the dark was another.

That first morning, I slid out of bed at three-fifteen a.m., trying not to wake Jerry and the kids. Without turning on any lights, I brushed my teeth, pulled my shoulder-length hair into a ponytail, and slipped on the T-shirt and jeans I'd set out the night before. I tiptoed downstairs, stepped into my thick-soled tennis shoes I'd left by the front door, crept out of the house into the starlight, and started my three-mile pedal to the bakery.

As I made my way down gravelly Company Creek Road and then onto the paved Stehekin Road, the only light to guide me came from the moon and the battery-operated headlight clamped onto the handlebars of my bike. There are no streetlights anywhere in Stehekin, and at three-thirty in the morning, all the houses I passed were dark.

There were no cars on the road at that hour either, and the quiet was as deep as in any Quaker meeting. I imagined the crackle of my tires through gravel waking a mother black bear, her brown eyes watching me, this possible threat to her cubs. I'd read backcountry guides about making noise when encountering bears; I hoped the jingling of the Minnie Mouse bell above my left handlebar grip would keep me safe.

Between the adrenalin of my pedaling and the possibility of meeting up with bears, snakes, or cougars, I was wide awake when I arrived at work. Even though the day's temperature might reach ninety, the early June night air brought pink to my cheeks and turned my fingers red. I pulled open the screen door at four a.m. on the dot.

Tammy, who lived with her preschool-aged son in a two-room apartment above the bakery, was already inside, rolling out dough for cinnamon rolls. Her brown braid reached to her waist and swayed back and forth as she stretched the dough the length of the bench—the golden, eight-foot long, chopping-block table that was center stage in the bakery. I slipped a bib apron over my head.

"Good morning, Tammy. Where do I start?"

Tammy smeared soft butter over the whole-wheat dough, sprinkled a heavy layer of cinnamon, brown sugar, and raisins, then rolled it all up and divided it with a serrated knife into neat, individual rounds. "Robbie'll be in soon," Tammy said, "so until she gets here, look through that black notebook at the recipes for scones and orange twists. That's probably what she'll have you start with."

I perched on the edge of a white plastic barrel filled with a hundred pounds of flour and paged through the notebook. I jotted notes in a little loose-leaf binder to help me remember which ingredients were kept in the bank of stainless steel refrigerators, each labeled with a number. Danish and focaccia doughs behind Door #1; eggs and butter behind Door #2. I double-checked quantities listed in the recipes, noting that many of the ingredients were in pounds instead of cups and that spices, salt, baking soda and baking powder amounts were in cups rather than teaspoons.

I thought back to countless orientations during my days in hospitals and clinics when, under the watchful eyes of more experienced head nurses, I worried I'd never remember where the bandages, bedpans, syringes, and catheters were stored. I had a case of new job jitters today, too, partly from my bicycle commute in the wilderness, but more out of worry that as a novice baker I wouldn't meet Robbie's high standards. The bakery was still chilly, but I was sweating when Robbie arrived.

"Hi Iris, glad you're here," she said, scribbling notes on the shopping list pinned to the bulletin board, grabbing an apron, and striding to the handwashing sink. Her hairstyle was identical to Tammy's, though Robbie's braid hung only to the middle of her back. "How was your bike ride?"

"Good. Didn't take as long as I expected, but I was pedaling pretty fast. I was afraid I might wake up some bears."

"Aw, don't let those bears scare you," Robbie snorted. "They're way more afraid of you than you are of them." I made a half-hearted attempt at a laugh and joined Robbie and Tammy behind the bench. "OK, let's get started on scones," Robbie said.

For the next two hours, Robbie and Tammy explained and demonstrated. I sketched diagrams and scrawled measurements in my little notebook for bear claws, hazelnut rolls, and croissants. Each entry included instructions about oven temperature and baking times, whether to use an egg wash or fruit glaze, and which fruits and nuts comprised the fillings for pastries. They showed me how to plop wedges of dough into the dented stainless steel scoop of a vintage scale so each loaf of bread and each bagel was the same size. I noted which ice cream scoop to use for cookie dough and which one for muffin batter.

Around six a.m., Robbie dropped bread slices into the toaster and cranked up the espresso machine for morning toast and coffee. With the help of caffeine and carbs, I felt ready to greet Robbie's husband, Cragg, and various of his four brothers who would stop in before opening time for a cup of coffee and some day-old baked goods. Tom, Mark, and Jim always offered smiles but rarely said more than "good morning" as they filled their coffee mugs from the thermos on the counter. Cliff typically had a story or joke to share. I would discover that Cragg usually lingered, as he did this morning, resting his football-player-sized frame on the wooden stool at the end of the glass display case.

"How're you doing this morning, Iris?" he said as he slid open the door of the case and snatched a muffin from a tray.

"Good, but I've got a lot to learn."

He looked over at Robbie and smiled; a dimple creased his left cheek and his blue eyes sparkled. "You didn't burn anything today, did you, Iris?"

"Nope, not yet," I said, imagining that my stumbles in my new job would be a source of entertainment in his household.

"OK, I guess we'll keep you on a while longer," he said, his grin turning into a chuckle. "Well, I better get to work. Now, Rob," he said, as he brushed past his wife on his way out the back door, "don't be too hard on Iris."

After our toast and coffee break, Robbie slid a Bonnie Raitt cassette in the tape deck and took up her post at the bench, rolling out piecrusts. Tammy took over instructing me in how to use the bakery's fifty-year-old Hobart floor model mixer. Its massive stainless steel bowl was big enough to knead dough for eight loaves of bread at a time. A sweeter mix, loaded with chunks of butter, yielded the dry ingredients for thirty-six

batches of scones. I counted to myself, trying to keep track of
when I had dumped enough flour, sugar, butter, and salt into
the bowl. Tammy demonstrated maneuvering the Hobart's
heavy steel gearshift to turn the five-pound paddle that mixed
the ingredients. Once the butter was in little bits and the mix
looked like corn meal, I put the gears in neutral and shut the
mixer off. Tammy clutched the handle on one side of the bowl,
and I gripped the other.

"One, two, three," Tammy said.

"Oomph!" we both said as we hoisted the bowl from the
mixer, staggered to the bench, and dumped out the contents.
For the next half hour, I weighed out the dry mix, filled plastic
bags with the quantity needed for a month's worth of scones,
and stacked the baggies in the freezer for use in the coming days.

"Time to scoop cookies," Robbie said, glancing at the clock
and sliding parchment paper onto a metal baking sheet big
enough to hold three dozen. Nearly halfway through my shift,
and I imagined Jerry and the kids were still asleep.

"The doughs are in those white buckets in fridge number
two," Robbie said. I pulled out tubs labeled chocolate chip, oat-
meal raisin, ginger, and snicker doodle.

"So, Iris…which scoop do you use for cookies?" Robbie asked.

"Umm," I said, thumbing through my notes, "the yellow one?"

"Nope, that's for muffins."

"Oh, right," I said, digging through the utensil crock for
a black-handled ice cream scoop. For each type of cookie, I
reached into the tubs, extracted little balls of chilled dough
with the scooper, and placed them on the sheets. My hands
sheened with butter after gently pressing the doughy spheres
into even circles.

"Set the timer for four minutes," Robbie said. "When it goes off, turn the pan and set the timer for another four. The dough will look under-baked, but that's the secret to chewy cookies."

For the next few hours, I dashed around the kitchen, sliding pans of bread dough and sheets of cookies and pastries in and out of the hot oven and onto the six-foot tall metal cooling rack. Timers beeped at intervals and Robbie ordered me to open the oven doors and rotate pans so everything baked evenly. Each shifting of pans warmed the air and infused it with smells of butter, sugar, cinnamon, fruit, and chocolate. As the sun rose, Robbie directed me to transfer bear claws, cinnamon rolls, sticky buns, muffins, scones, and croissants onto trays and antique plates for the display case.

By the time I flipped over the open sign outside the bakery's screened-in front porch at eight a.m., my T-shirt was damp with sweat, my back was aching, and a small burn on my forearm stung from a collision with a hot pan. My perspiring temples throbbed with the timelines and techniques Robbie had peppered me with during the previous four hours. As a nurse, I knew how critical it was to give the right dose of a medication at the right time, but I hadn't expected a similar demand for precision in the bakery. Just as I began to wonder if I wanted that kind of pressure, I pictured myself at that hour if I were still working at the health department—soothing a crying infant after giving vaccines, interviewing people about when they'd last eaten at a restaurant where a worker had hepatitis, or tallying patient visits to the immunization clinic. Gratitude erased my headache.

Within minutes of opening, locals and tourists started streaming in. Customers practically shouted, "Mmm, it smells so good in here." I grinned, and noticed Robbie roll her eyes at Tammy, even as a half-smile escaped. She probably was accustomed to the praise, but I'd never heard that comment any place I'd worked as a nurse.

Later that morning, sweaty, dirt-caked hikers stopped in after being picked up at a trailhead by the Park Service shuttle bus. Waffle-soled boots and bulging backpacks weighed down their lean frames, most of their body fat depleted after trudging for weeks on the Pacific Crest Trail and eating only dehydrated food.

"Wow! Are we glad you're here. We've been thinking about sticky buns for ten miles," one hiker said as he placed his order. "Uh, would you put that gooey part that's stuck on the pan on my plate, too?" he asked.

I would think of these appreciative comments from customers often in the coming months as I unraveled my disillusionment with nursing. Troubled pregnant women with complex needs don't always welcome a public health nurse's help. During E. coli outbreaks and measles epidemics, the public views you with suspicion or fear.

After the morning breakfast rush, Tammy and Robbie taught me how to make the bakery's lunch items—pizzas and pizza pockets. Here was another chance to weigh dough (one-and-a-half pounds for pizza and two pounds for the pockets) and roll it out. I learned which fridge held the tomato sauce, cheeses, and toppings and how thick to layer it all on. Tammy demonstrated how to brush an egg wash on all the edges of the pizza pocket dough, spread sauce over half of the dough, sprinkle a layer of mozzarella cheese, fold the plain half over the filling, and pinch the edges together. A final egg wash on the top, five diagonal slits with a knife through the top layer of dough, and the pocket was ready for the oven. Seven hours into my shift, the bakery's sweet scents were replaced with oregano, garlic, onions, and peppers.

The regulars knew when the pizzas came out, and they lined up to get the first slices with the melted mozzarella stringing over the freshly cut edges. I slid the first one, dripping with sausage, mushrooms, olives, and onions, off the baking pan and onto the wooden chopping block.

"Cut that into eighteen equal pieces," Robbie said.

I squinted my right eye shut, notched the dough with the knife and glided it the length of the pizza.

"That's crooked as hell, Iris," Robbie said.

My face warmed as I looked up at her, then returned my gaze to the cut veering toward the pizza's lower left corner. "Sorry about that."

"Well, just don't let it happen again," Robbie said, the corners of her mouth slightly curving upward. I would come to learn that was her signal she was making a joke.

With just a few minutes before clocking out, I discovered there was one more task to be done.

"Time to scrape the floor," Robbie said.

"Scrape the floor?" I asked, noticing for the first time clumps of butter and flour and bits of berries and onions smooshed onto the cream-colored linoleum.

"Yep, it's the last thing we do every morning," Tammy said, slipping off her apron. "Here's a bench knife you can use." She slid one of the tools across the wooden tabletop and clutched another one in her right hand. "I'll show you."

I picked up the four-inch wide rectangular implement by its wooden handle. It's not really a knife, though it does have a wide, dull blade. I had used one earlier in the morning to cut raw dough into hunks so I could weigh it for bread and had slid it underneath warm pastries to transfer them onto cooling racks. Now I watched as Tammy knelt down on the floor in front of the refrigerators, grasped the handle, and used the blade to loosen the ground-in food bits.

"I'll keep going here," Tammy said, "and you can start over by the case. We'll meet in the middle."

I got down on all fours and angled the blade so it would lift the debris from the floor. My ponytail flopped down over my shoulder as I scraped and inched backward. After a few minutes, I leaned back on the heels of my tennis shoes, massaged my lower back, and contemplated my spot on the floor, looking up at the counter and the stovetop. The baking had been demanding, but fun; I hadn't expected this assignment. I can't say I enjoyed it, but I knew it was something I had to do. I didn't want to leave a mess for the staff who would work the rest of the day and for the person who would mop the floor at closing so it would be spotless the next morning when we bakers arrived. We made the mess; we should at least help to clean it up.

I felt I had been brought to my knees as a nurse, humbled and disappointed and under-valued. Had I left my job without cleaning up the mess of my confusion about nursing, health care, and the public health bureaucracy I was part of? This end-of-shift duty symbolized the internal labor I needed to do. On my knees. In prayer, seeking and opening myself to whatever work I'd be led to.

After intersecting with Tammy beneath the bench, I stood up slowly and brushed flour from my knees. From where I stood, it seemed it wasn't just the mingled scents of warm butter, cinnamon, and brown sugar that enticed people into the bakery. A stop there granted a practice session in putting the heart's desires first. Perhaps this new job, floor scraping and all, would help me adopt the bakery's motto for my life as well.

"Good work today, Iris," Robbie said as I washed the floor's grime from my palms. "Get yourself something to eat before you go, and I'll see you in the morning."

I grabbed a slice of pizza and slouched in a chair on the bakery porch. Alone there, in a lull between breakfast and lunch, I savored the spice of sausage chunks, the tang of tomato sauce, the customers' appreciation and Robbie's acknowledgment. I massaged my neck and thought about the cool shower and nap I'd indulge in when I got home.

I wasn't ready to literally eat dessert first. I slid a chocolate chip cookie into a paper bag and stuffed it into my backpack along with my little notebook full of baking instructions. I rode my bike home more slowly, my Minnie Mouse bell jingling its greeting to the bears still hidden in the forest.

CHAPTER 9

Wildfire Season

SMOKE ROLLED INTO THE STEHEKIN VALLEY like an ocean fog, blanketing us in wintry gray. But this was July, barely one month after our move, and the haze oozing into our new home was from wildfires, not the Puget Sound marine air we were accustomed to.

Wildfire season arrived in the North Cascades after a two-week run of rainless, one-hundred-degree days and lightning strikes in the nearby Okanogan National Forest. The blazes dropped a thick, dingy curtain on the shoreline, but despite the haze and smoldering campfire smell, the *Lady of the Lake* kept sailing. Her crew brought news that a crack of lightning can change lives—ski slopes in Leavenworth in blazes, and three hundred people evacuated from the town of Chelan.

The thunder and lightning storms of my Midwest upbring-
ing must have immunized me from fear when lightning cracked
in ridges above the Stehekin Valley, because I wasn't aware that
we in Stehekin were in danger until a community meeting on
July 29. Someone from nearly every Stehekin household came
to the Golden West Visitor Center. People scooted their chairs
over worn, hardwood floors for a better view of the National
Forest Service map propped on an easel. Two thumbtack-sized
black circles marked fires at nearby Rainbow Ridge and Little
Boulder. A banana-shaped mark stretched over Purple Mountain. Butte Creek was blackened, too.

This was our first meeting with Alan Hoffmeister, one
of the many specialists from the National Park Service who
would come to Stehekin to try to outmaneuver the fires. Alan
looked over the faces in the crowd, his index finger steadily
pointing to the four darkened areas on the map. "Although the
fires are several miles away," he said, "they've already encom-
passed a thousand acres and are burning erratically."

He predicted pines and firs, parched from diminished snow
melt and eight years of drought, might burst into flame and roll
down dehydrated ridges, spreading the firestorm into the Boulder Creek drainage area just a mile northwest of us. "If necessary, fire crews and equipment will be brought to Stehekin by
boat or air. We're doing everything possible to stop the fires."

A couple of neighbors shook their heads. I heard someone
mutter, "Yeah, right."

Cool sweat prickled my hairline, and I noticed Alan swallow hard. As I listened to him acknowledge that other fires
across the west were taxing firefighting resources, I heard my
own voice just a year earlier in Bellingham when I'd faced that
group of parents grieving the death of a child from E. coli infec-

tion. As the county health department's communicable disease supervisor, I met with families at the childcare center the toddler attended. Then, I was the one who swallowed hard before describing the health department's investigation and prevention efforts. "We're doing all we can to get this infection under control," I told them. Murmurings of fear and doubt had rippled through the childcare room.

But tonight, I was in the audience, straining for reassurance that Alan and all the other "experts" could keep us safe. My cold sweat was for him—and for us.

Then Alan suggested that, even though evacuation was unlikely, we should begin thinking about it. Nervous laughter floated through the cramped room as he encouraged us each to pack a single bag weighing no more than seventy-five pounds, the same amount airlines allowed then for checked luggage. I searched the faces of the long-time Stehekinites in the crowd, trying to read their expressions. Were they worried? Scared?

"These fires are more fierce than at any time ever in this region," Alan said. "You might have as little as fifteen minutes to catch a boat to leave. Don't wait for an evacuation notice to pack."

At home after the meeting, I looked around the log cabin's large open bedroom our family shared. Some of our treasured possessions were in storage, but many were in that room— worn baby blankets Rachel and Matt still snuggled under at night, boxes of photos I planned to organize into albums, the flute I'd owned since third grade, and a quilt we'd received as a wedding gift. I imagined the pages of our already bulging family journal curled and charred. I set out the four biggest duffel bags I could find.

Not wanting to alarm the kids, Jerry and I emphasized Alan's reassurance that evacuation was unlikely. "Just pack like you're going to Grandma's for a weekend," Jerry said as he supervised Rachel and Matt loading their bags.

As I sorted, I ticked off treasures that would put us over the weight limit—our broken-in hiking boots, cross-country skis, my yellow bicycle with the Minnie Mouse bell, and the Kitchen Aid mixer. Would they be there when we returned from evacuation? My stomach tightened over nature's threat to our idyllic retreat. I knew I had lessons to learn in the wilderness, but I hadn't anticipated this exercise in condensing my family's life into four bags.

Then I thought of our neighbors who had even more at stake. Robbie's bakery, Cragg's road-grading and snow-removal equipment, the horses for their pack trips. Wally's mother's A-frame where we'd hatched our dream of living in Stehekin. Jean's art studio packed to the rafters with fabric for quilted wall hangings. The little cabin Jean shared with her husband, Jonathan, and their son Mugs, and the handcrafted house Jonathan was building for them.

"Are you scared?" I'd asked Jean as we walked to our cars after the community meeting.

"Hell yes," she said. "I'm gonna' get Jonathan and Mugs to string all of our garden hoses around the studio and the new house."

"What about your cabin?"

"It's falling down anyway. But the other places, well, we can't lose them."

I barreled through our packing with no idea how, or if, anyone could keep us safe.

That night, images of a cyclone of fire intruded into my

sleep. Every sound in the dark mimicked the crackle and hiss that I imagined echoing through the forest. Jerry snored softly beside me, and I could hear the kids rustling in their beds. What a fool I'd been to expose our family to these dangers. During our years of visiting Stehekin, I'd learned that the potential for natural disasters is part of everyday life here. Nearly everyone had stories of floods, fires, avalanches, and backcountry accidents that had destroyed property and claimed friends and family. Firs scorched by lightning marked the cycles of their lives. Now I was experiencing this reality first-hand, faced with a situation I couldn't control. I tried to loosen my grip with deep breathing and prayers.

I was hoping for the kind of calm I'd felt fourteen years earlier when I awaited results of my pregnancy test. Jerry and I had known we wanted children someday, maybe five years into our marriage. When I missed a period soon after our first anniversary, I went to the bathroom hourly. I kept hoping for a spot of blood, for proof that our birth control was still working and that my period was merely late. Jerry and I had both just been accepted into schools—the University of Washington graduate nursing program for me and the sign language interpreter-training program at Seattle Central Community College for him. Our planning for a cross-country move that summer did not include the prospect of an infant. For the first time since the onset of puberty, I longed for the twinge in my lower back and the cramp in my belly that signaled my period.

Too anxious to wait until a urine test would give accurate results, I asked for a blood test to confirm if I was pregnant or not. The night before I'd get the lab report, I replayed the conversations Jerry and I had had about what we would do if the test turned out positive. We agreed I wouldn't have an abortion, but we couldn't go any further with the implications. With fears swirling through my mind about my ability to parent, questions about whether I could proceed with graduate school, and doubts about moving to Seattle, I decided to pray. I silently asked God to lead me, us, through whatever news the next day would bring. Tears trickled toward my pillow as I breathed in and out deeply, slowly, telling God I was turning this over. Soon I felt a calm, a presence, and an assurance I had never experienced before. It carried me through the phone call from my doctor's office the next day and the move to Seattle. And, it was there for me in my third trimester of pregnancy when an ultrasound showed twins.

Now, in Stehekin, I again sought that assurance.

Sleep finally came, and a gentle wind during the night sent the smoke another direction. The next day's clear dawn made it easy to forget the force devouring forests just a few miles away. The respite was brief. Within hours, neon-yellow fliers describing the "Stehekin Evacuation Contingency Plan" blanketed the valley. National Park Service rangers had hand-delivered the bulletins; with no phones, and no television or radio transmission, the pony express-like system was the only way to get the word out.

I tried to gauge the real danger by locals' comments when they stopped in the bakery that morning. Wally grunted as usual when he filled up his plastic coffee mug. "It's just another fire," he growled.

Robbie muttered as she re-wrote the bakery grocery list, crossing off some items and decreasing quantities of others.

"I heard they had to shut down Stevens Pass because of smoke," she said. "There goes our tourist business."

The afternoon arrival of Mike Monahan, a national fire commander from Utah, signaled this wasn't "just another fire." At the Golden West that night, the worried-looking, red-haired official outlined for the local crowd the challenge of preventing the small fires nearby from combining into one large one.

"Several factors complicate our situation here," he said. "First, we can't send crews to the fires, not even our most experienced hot shots, because there aren't escape routes in the area." I nodded, remembering reports in early July of the deaths of fourteen such expert firefighters on Storm King Mountain in Colorado. "Second," he went on, "we can't use fire retardant aircraft, except helicopters, in the steep terrain. But, with all the fires we've had in the past few weeks, teams are using helicopters all across the west; we have to wait our turn."

Monahan's words left me feeling almost as vulnerable as the squad trapped when the Colorado fire took an unexpected turn. Lake Chelan, always my route to tranquility, could be my only escape from disaster.

Although there were fewer tourists, firefighters from Mississippi and Georgia doubled our population, working alongside locals to clear fallen pine needles and branches throughout our community. If wildfires cascaded from ridges above us, we didn't want fuel waiting to turn them into house fires. Barges delivered red fire engines and miles of hose that crews snaked around the two shops, the Lodge, the post office, the Ranger Station, and the Visitor Center. Gasoline-fueled pumps, also shipped in, stood ready to draw water from the lake if the fire above rolled into "Downtown Stehekin." We suspended community baseball games when the diamond became home to a different team's gear—orange fireproof tents, bright yellow helmets, and compact shovels.

The fire crews kept the bakery busy; their managers con-
tracted with us for their lunches. The loaves of bread and pastries we made every day went into seventy brown bags packed
with peanut butter and jelly sandwiches, herb bagels, black
bottom cupcakes, and ginger cookies. A couple of crew members would stop in each morning, their fluorescent yellow long-
sleeved shirts stained with sweat and their faces caked with
dust, to pick up the lunches. The Southerners would drawl
their thanks around mouthfuls of maple bars.

The crews also fueled up at breakfast and dinner each day
at the Ranch. Since both the Ranch and the Stehekin Pastry
Company were run by two of the Courtney brothers and their
families, they communicated via two-way radio across the
seven miles between their operations. Usually, chatter from
the black box entertained us at the bakery while we rolled out
croissant dough and loaded toppings on pizza. One morning
early in August, as thunder rumbled outside, the radio crackled
with Cliff's voice.

Robbie turned up the volume just as her brother-in-law
shouted, "Lightning struck SiSi Ridge!"

"Where's SiSi Ridge?" I asked as I shaped Danish pastries.

"About a mile up behind your house," Robbie said. Our
house—Cliff's home he had rented to us for the summer. No
wonder his usually playful voice sounded so tense.

As I fretted about my family's whereabouts, I nearly forgot
to add eggs to the blackberry scones. Jerry had to be hearing
the same news I was because he was working for Cliff that day,
driving the shuttle bus the nine miles between the Landing and
the Ranch. The kids had been in the bakery earlier on their
way to take our mail to the post office, so I knew they were safe
from fire action near our house. Still, I eavesdropped on the

brothers' debates about hiking up the ridge to fight the fire as I absentmindedly sliced the scones into triangles.

"We're in luck," Cliff reported a few hours later. "Monahan says a helicopter's on the way."

At the end of my shift, I retreated to a public dock to watch a red-and-white Sikorsky Sky Crane, a military-style helicopter, pull water from the lake. A bucket, swinging on a rope from the chopper's belly, hauled up two thousand gallons of water with each dip. All afternoon it showered me as water slopped on its way to the flames on the peaks above. The rhythmic whirl of rotors was both unsettling and comforting. Runs every fifteen minutes throughout the rest of the day squelched the blaze at Si Si Ridge.

The report at that night's community meeting was as feared; fire had advanced to Boulder Creek, just a couple miles from where we sat on the valley floor. That inferno demanded two helicopters, eight hours a day, to cool it down enough so fire crews could get up there. After a few days of water drops, Mike Monahan told us the fire at Boulder Creek was too widespread and hot for crews to extinguish.

"It won't go out completely until snow falls," he said.

The next day at work, trying to convince myself that I could handle life in the wilderness, I tried to imitate my co-workers' casual attitudes. I grumbled to Robbie, "So much for a fun-filled Stehekin summer."

"You just never know around here," she said, her gaze focused on the pastries I was arranging on serving platters.

Some days over the next few weeks, the smoke cleared to reveal blue skies. Two sets of friends visited, the kids rode their bikes to the landing to swim, Jerry shuttled a few tourists between the Ranch and the bakery, and the mail and groceries arrived on *The Lady.* We became the new home for Boris, a tabby that was part of a local litter, and Skoshi, a gray kitten with a crooked tail that friends from Bellingham had hiked into Stehekin in a fanny pack. The two felines spun around in circles and snoozed in a curl on the couch, and I persuaded myself that the "experts" would save us.

Other days, we'd hear the helicopters again, smoke would fill the valley again, and my fear—that this place and way of life would be destroyed—returned. One day in mid-August we ventured out on a hike, only to be turned back by signs proclaiming "Fire Danger—Trail Closed." During dinner that evening, Jerry proposed a different activity.

"I heard Phil and Brun Garfoot talking about going to the gravel pit at night to watch the fires burning above Boulder Creek," he said. "They say it's quite a show."

"Let's check it out," Matt said, dumping his dishes in the sink and stuffing his feet into his tennis shoes without bothering to tie the laces. All four of us climbed into the Suburban and headed down valley.

We were the only ones sitting on the mounds of rock and sand that night, and I wondered if we newcomers were the targets of a little practical joke by our seasoned friends. We talked quietly in the warm darkness as growing numbers of stars brightened the sky.

"Where would we see anything *if* it's going to happen?" I asked Jerry. Just as he pointed to the northwest, a burst of orange exploded into the blackness, followed shortly by another right next to it.

"Whoa!" we said in unison.

"So that's what they mean by crowning," Jerry said. The trees had been smoldering for days, building up so much heat

that flames shot out through the tops, causing the tips to ex-
plode, fly off, and light nearby treetops.

"I think nature is reminding us who's in charge," I whispered, recalling the Sky Cranes dousing the forest all day long.
"It's hard to accept our powerlessness."

I thought I knew about powerlessness. I had felt it many
times during twenty years of nursing—cancers that didn't respond to chemicals or radiation, infections that resisted antibiotics, women who returned to abusive relationships, teens who
played Russian roulette with sex and drugs. Now, streaks of
yellow-orange spearing silently into the darkness gave me another lesson about control.

Bits of gravel tumbled as Jerry stood up and stretched his
hand to me, tugging me to my feet.

"OK, guys," he said to the kids, "time to head home."

Rains in late August weakened the fire's strength. We unpacked our evacuation bags and re-packed boxes to move into
the house we'd rent from the Barnharts through the school
year. Mike Monahan moved on to manage a different fire. Another Incident Commander directed mop-up efforts, and local Park Service employees handled flare-ups that waxed and
waned all through September. By the first week of October, the
fire-fighting teams rolled up the hoses and barged them out,
along with their shovels, axes, tents, and trucks. After weeks of
being prepared for fire on our doorsteps, these tools of protection disappeared, leaving in their place a deeper understanding: no matter how hard I worked, I couldn't eliminate all the
threats to life any more than Mike Monahan could end the fire
at Boulder Creek.

I awakened one morning in mid-October to a white glisten
on McGregor Mountain, just visible through the living room

window. Fortunately, the season's first snow had come early; the tension in my neck eased with this proof that the fires were over—at least for this year.

CHAPTER 10

Not Getting Along is Not an Option

There was no need to set my alarm to wake Rachel and Matt for their first day at the Stehekin School. A half hour before mine was scheduled to buzz, the two kids were creating their own buzz in the kitchen, making peanut butter and jelly sandwiches and rustling through the cupboard for paper bags.

"Matt, quit juggling the apples and put one in your lunch," I heard Rachel say as I slipped on my robe and headed for the kitchen.

"Good morning, guys. Excited about your first day?"

"Yay," they shouted in unison.

While the two of them crunched granola and gulped orange juice, I went back to the bedroom to get dressed. My mind wandered to the day seven years earlier when I'd put them on a bus for the hour-long ride to kindergarten in Seattle's inner city. We had walked together to the bus stop a block from our house, each of the kids wearing backpacks that reached from their shoulders to their knees. Matt's wispy blond hair refused to lie flat, and Rachel had a big gap where a front tooth had been. They marched up the steps of the bus and shared a seat a few rows behind the driver. Rachel's oval chin and wide smile barely cleared the bottom edge of the bus window as she waved good-bye; my chin crumpled.

Here, there was no bus service, and the kids could have ridden their bikes the three miles to the school. But with fewer work hours now that the tourist season was waning, Jerry and I both had the day off, so at seven-thirty a.m., we all piled into Colonel Mustard. As the car rumbled across Harlequin Bridge, I stuffed my chilled hands into the pockets of my polar fleece jacket and gazed at the banks of the Stehekin up toward Mc-Gregor. Sunshine lit up the yellow, orange, and red of the vine maples and dogwoods; they sparkled like jewels among the pines and firs scaling up from the valley floor.

The minute Jerry put his foot on the brake in the school driveway, the kids scooted out of the backseat and jogged up the steps of the schoolhouse porch. Mr. Scutt (the way we would refer to the teacher, Ron, now that school was in session) leaned against the railing. "Rachel and Matt, Welcome!" he boomed as he reached out to shake their hands.

Jerry and I followed the kids into the main classroom where I noticed small bouquets of dahlias and zinnias on a table in the front of the room. Fifteen wooden-top desks formed a horseshoe. Matt and Rachel skirted the semi-circle until they found the desks labeled with their names.

One of the many attractions to Stehekin for us had been this one-room, kindergarten-through-eighth grade public school. We'd read about the early history of education in the valley in Carol Stone's book, *Stehekin: Glimpses from the Past.* The first teacher came to Stehekin in the 1890s. Many years, classes had met only in the summer when downlake teachers came for vacation. When the "old school" was built in 1921, the school year continued on through February, then closed until spring. In those days, no one plowed the snow off the roads. The summer before we moved to Stehekin, Jerry and the kids and I had poked around in that building, now preserved as a museum.

We'd also stopped in at the "new school," built in 1988, and admired the students' drawings, paintings, and writings posted on the log walls. Although described as a one-room school, the log building has several rooms besides the main classroom. The first floor's "motion room," with its shiny tile floor and cathedral ceiling, is the perfect spot for painting, swinging on the rope suspended from a log beam, and playing recorders. Upstairs is a library and computer area. But the main classroom is the heart of the building, and it's where the kids spend most of the school day. That's where we picked up a copy of the annual school newspaper, *The Way Through.* Produced by the older students, its twenty-four pages featured students' stories, drawings, and photos. Now, Rachel and Matt were taking their own places in the school's story.

"See you at two o'clock," I said to the kids after giving each a quick kiss on the cheek.

"Bye, Mom," Rachel whispered back as she circled my shoulders in a hug.

"See ya," Matt said, stuffing his backpack under his chair.

Back at home, Jerry tackled the pile of logs he'd been splitting for our winter heating supply, and I chopped onions and
peppers for tomato sauce and the lasagna we'd have for a first-
day-of-school celebratory dinner. While the sauce simmered
and the noodles boiled, I thought about what Ron had told us
earlier in the summer about what the kids could expect.

"I like the students to wake up first and not go right into
academics," he said. "After a time of singing or jumping rope in
the motion room, they gather in the main classroom for a half
hour of sharing. They always have things to share," Ron said. I
wondered what Rachel and Matt would share with their new
classmates and what we'd hear when they got home.

That night, they talked non-stop through dinner, cleanup,
and into the evening. They told us how the younger students
had presented the bouquets I'd seen that morning.

"Justin handed a bunch to me," Rachel said "and then he
giggled and said, 'Welcome to Stehekin School.' He's so cute."

"Libby got flowers, too, because she's in eighth grade," Matt
said. "You saw how the desks were in a U shape, right?"

Jerry and I nodded and grinned at the volley of explanations.

"Well, the younger kids sit in the desks in the middle, and
the older ones are on the sides. Since Libby's the oldest she got
the desk in the far right back corner. It's the best one, because
that means you've been there the longest."

"Yeah, she's the Queen of the Roost," Rachel said. "She's
been here forever."

"Great lasagna," Matt said.

"In a couple weeks we're going on a hike to Horseshoe Basin," Rachel said.

"We're gonna learn all about mines and stuff," Matt added.

Jerry and I had been to Horseshoe Basin just a month

earlier while the kids were at camp in Oregon with other Quaker teens. Situated in a large cirque between Ripsaw Ridge and Sahale, Boston, and Buckner Mountains, the trail ends at the abandoned Black Warrior Mine. Waterfalls cascade down from the snow and ice fields above, creating frigid pools where we skinny-dipped on that hot afternoon. I trusted that the school outing would involve more exploring of the old mine than we had done and would omit the naked swim.

When the kids had returned from that Quaker campout, Matt's T-shirt still hung loose around his neck, but his voice seemed a little deeper. I sensed something different in Rachel, too. Once at home, she told me that her period had started on her way to camp.

"Some of my friends had supplies with them," she said, "so they helped me."

"Oh, honey," I said, hugging her petite frame to me. "Congratulations," was the only word I could get out around the lump in my throat.

Rachel might have stepped one toe into adulthood, but it was obvious that most of her was still in childhood as she described recess that first day at the Stehekin School. Its playground, a grassy meadow, butts up against the forested mountainside behind the school.

"Officially, recess is at eleven," she said, "but that's when we eat lunch, so that during lunchtime, at twelve-thirty, we can play outside for a whole hour." Another privilege their eighthgrade friend Libby had was to be in charge of kids on the playground. Rachel and Matt described how she organized them into teams for a soccer game.

"And in the winter," Matt said, "we can sled during recess. Libby says the snow gets really deep on the hill behind the school."

What a contrast this first day at Stehekin School was to the start of school for Rachel and Matt just a year earlier. After the fire destroyed Kulshan before it even opened, they had been scrunched into Whatcom Middle School with its nine hundred sixth-, seventh-, and eighth-graders. Rachel's class was housed in a portable room that seemed to invite withdrawal; Matt's, in the basement, was like a hideout where he and his buddies could scheme ways to sidestep the rules. I wondered if they'd both revel in the isolation of Stehekin and the intimacy of its close-knit school or if Rachel would shrink and Matt rebel.

*   *   *

"NOT GETTING ALONG IS NOT AN OPTION," Ron had told me when I asked him what it was like to teach in a small school. "The children and I must get along. I must find a way to make this happen," he had said. I knew my children, and I'd met most of the kids at the school; I couldn't imagine that getting along was much of a problem. Then, one day near the end of September, we found a letter in our mailbox from Ron, asking for a conference.

Matt should be able to explain the purpose of this meeting, Ron had written, *but in short, I am finding him to be argumentative and disruptive in class. He is a good boy at heart, but we have to get some things straight before going further.*

We'd been there with Matt before, too. Our conversations often went like this:

Me: "Matt, I told you I wanted you to deal with the laundry in the dryer when you came home from school.

Matt: "But you didn't say I should fold it."

Me: "You're right, but I didn't expect it would end up in a lump in the laundry basket. Do I have to tell you every step?"

Matt: "But you said..."

We'd heard him and Rachel go round and round, too, Matt sounding like a lawyer arguing a case before the Supreme Court. But still, Ron's letter stung.

I recalled the image I'd seen of Ron one day when I'd lingered after dropping the kids off. He'd eased his towering body into a large canvas chair at the front of the classroom to read aloud, his reading glasses perched slightly below the bridge of his nose. When one of the students shared a funny story about swimming in the lake, Ron threw back his head, laughed from his belly, and slapped his knee.

"The goal is to get him to laugh," Rachel would say, and often she or Matt had an example of what had worked that day. We didn't know until we got the letter that Matt wasn't having much success getting Mr. Scutt to laugh.

In the weeks following Ron's letter, changes were almost too subtle to detect at the time. At the Stehekin School, Matt could move at the pace he was ready for academically and could pursue some of his interests, such as the stars and the universe, while still having time to juggle and finish up childhood. Perhaps it was the expectation that, as one of the older students, he had a responsibility to model the desired behavior for younger students; at home we relied on him too, for wood-splitting and help with other chores to keep the household going.

Whatever methods Mr. Scutt used, he and Matt did "get some things straight." One day after school, Matt waved a folded square of yellow lined paper under my nose. I recognized Ron's script bleeding through the yellow and searched Matt's face for signs of distress. As I unfolded the sheet, I noticed the corners of Matt's mouth curve up. Mine did, too, when I scanned Ron's comments. *I truly appreciate your thoughtful participation*, it read. *You asked thought-provoking (rather than simply provoking) questions and seemed to really immerse yourself into the concepts we studied.*

Rachel had a different approach to getting along, and Mr. Scutt picked up on it during class discussions about the characters and moral dilemmas in *The Adventures of Huckleberry Finn*. He wrote to her, *I always found myself hungering to hear more from you, but the rate of conversation by some of the other students was so fast and enlivened that I think you sometimes sat back and retreated from the field. Is that true?*

This behavior was familiar to me, too, not because I'd seen it so much in Rachel, but because it was how I often responded in situations when I knew my views were different from others. I'd done it as a child when I didn't want to upset my mom by disagreeing with her. Later, in early adulthood, when my path diverged sharply from hers, I withdrew. I feared she would reject me.

Quaker teachings of the value of each person, and the importance of listening for the wisdom we all have access to, had fostered openness to different perspectives than those I'd grown up with. Those same beliefs, though, often left me feeling uncertain of what it was I considered to be true and still fearful that if I expressed it, I'd be disliked. Much like Rachel, I spent my early months in Stehekin sitting back and listening.

Like at my first meeting of the Craft Cabin Co-operative members. Throughout the summer I'd experimented with collage and watercolors and had taken lessons in linoleum block printing with a local artist. Jean, an officer in the co-op, cheered on my fledgling art exploration and had invited me to the meeting to learn more about how the co-op ran. "You've made a good start with block printing," Jean had said. "Maybe you could make some prints and cards to sell in the Craft Cabin."

I'd slammed the back door when I got home. "How was the meeting?" Jerry had asked as I reached for the bottle of ibuprofen in the kitchen cabinet.

"Frustrating. Hardly anybody showed up, and there was no agenda. Then, when people started questioning what kind of merchandise is acceptable and how much of the work has to be done here in Stehekin, I discovered there were no guidelines for any of this." I yanked the cold-water faucet, filled a glass, and washed down two pills.

"You're a good facilitator. Did you say anything?"

"Nope. I was afraid to. I don't want to be one of those outsiders who comes in and tries to run things. And I don't want to piss people off so they don't want me to be involved."

"I think people can handle hearing your opinions," Jerry said.

"Maybe," I said, "but you know how I hate it when I'm the one who disagrees. I wish I could be more like Jean and just say what I think and trust that people won't reject me."

I had a similar worry a few weeks later at the public hearing for a new management plan for North Cascades National Park. The plan's limits on collecting wood and using pack horses concerned many in Stehekin, but the issue that pulled eighty people to the Golden West that night was the proposal to close the most distant part of the Stehekin Road to vehicles. The closure would add another twelve miles to many hikes in the backcountry, including the trek our family had done five years earlier over Cascade Pass. We probably wouldn't have attempted it if we hadn't been able to get a Park Service shuttle to drive us those last twelve miles into Stehekin.

Some at the meeting expressed concern for the impact of the road on the valley's fragile ecosystem; others argued for greater ease to experience the wild beauty here. Just as with the forest fires, I recognized my limited understanding of the complexities of environmental protection and personal land use rights. Although I didn't know the specifics here, I did know from working in state and county government that public policy and private interests often clash. I also knew that here, with private land and businesses intermingled with a national park, those conflicts co-existed among neighbors, and within families. I listened closely, my heart racing. Closure of the road would make the anticipated annual day hike to Horseshoe Basin impossible for the Stehekin School kids. Finally, I rose and appealed to the Park Superintendent to keep this option available. Though I was among the majority that night, I knew that others would be disappointed in my opposition to the preservation plan. I wondered if speaking up was worth the risk of alienating people I liked, respected, and would rely on in this remote place.

Perhaps, in the coming year, both Rachel and I would learn to let people hear our voices.

*   *   *

ONCE SCHOOL HAD STARTED, the bakery cut back its hours to Thursday through Sunday through the middle of October. Rachel had joined the crew as our dishwasher on the weekends, and I worked as much as ever because one of the full-time bakers had left after Labor Day. By then, I felt I'd gotten into the swing of baking and that my bear claws, raspberry rolls, and orange twists finally met Robbie's high standards. I hadn't expected there'd be a final exam, though.

The Thursday before the bakery closed for the season, Tammy was too sick to work, and a bug had hit Robbie, too. Robbie slogged to the bakery to mix doughs for bread and cinnamon rolls and scoop batter into muffin tins.

"Sorry to leave you like this," she said as she scrawled notes for me about other pastries for the day.

"I'll do what I can," I said, "but it won't be the same as when you and Tammy are here. Thank goodness the Ranch doesn't need pies."

"Yeah, I wouldn't do that to you, but you'll do great with everything else," Robbie said as she hobbled out the back door. "You're a pro now."

With such high praise from Robbie, I managed to fill the case with cinnamon rolls, scones, muffins, cookies, and pizza (no longer "crooked as hell"). I took extra care with my favorites—the orange twists—wanting to show off the skill I'd developed twirling the buttery dough.

"I feel good about being able to do all that baking by myself," I told Jerry that night as I soaked my feet in a pan of steamy water. "But I'm glad it was just for one day."

My solo bake was just a warm-up for my final days on the job, though. The last weekend the bakery was open was as busy as any summer day with locals stocking up on baked goods and special orders for their freezers. The next day, Robbie opened the bakery to the entire school. The bench hummed with the kids forming cinnamon rolls, pizza, and French bread in shapes from dragons to daisies.

As I transferred the creations onto baking sheets and slid them into the oven, Robbie set out dishes of cream cheese frosting, chocolate chips, nuts, raisins, and coconut. Tammy placed a carrot cupcake in front of each student. I watched Rachel and Matt shift into their older student roles, guiding the younger ones and praising their imaginative efforts.

That night as the kids packed their lunches, they told us they wanted to start getting to school by seven thirty.

"But it doesn't start until eight," I said.

"Yeah, but Mr. Scutt says he gets up at four fifteen every morning," Matt said, "and he's usually at school by five thirty."

"He likes the quiet time to get ready for the day," Rachel said as she sliced carrots and put them in a baggie. "He said it's okay for us to come early if we want to read. And next year," she said, sliding her lunch bag into the refrigerator, "when we're eighth graders, we can help get the room ready for the day."

My eyes widened as I looked across the counter at Jerry. He swallowed a smile.

"Or we can do our jobs," Matt said. "Mugs and I signed up to chop kindling for the woodstove, and he comes at seven thirty. So, Rachel and I are gonna ride our bikes tomorrow and meet Mugs at the bridge."

After the kids went upstairs to their rooms, I motioned to Jerry to follow me into our bedroom and to close the door.

"I guess Rachel's changed her mind about just one year," I whispered.

"Sounds like it. What do you think of a second year?"

"It's what I'd hoped for from the beginning," I said. "It makes sense for the kids to finish their elementary school years here, and I'd love to go through all the seasons a second time. What about you?"

"Yep. We've already done the hard part with our Clearness Committee and finding jobs and a house during the school year. It's nice to think we won't have to leave next summer." Apparently we'd all made progress in getting along.

First Snow

I SAT IN A PLASTIC CHAIR NEXT TO THE DESK that had once been mine at the health department; I noticed a pile of papers spilling out of the in-box and the stack of pink message slips tucked under the corner of the phone. Carole, the child health supervisor who had added my communicable disease program duties to hers when my supervisor position had been eliminated the year before, looked up from her open appointment book. Names and places inked every line.

"How's it feel to be back?" Carole asked.

After four months of pre-dawn baking, it had felt both strange and familiar to stride through the chilling October mist in Bellingham and into the lobby of the county health department. Instead of butter and cinnamon, a faint smell of rubbing alcohol wafted in the air. It was my first time back since we'd moved to Stehekin. That day, I was there not as a full-time staff nurse but as a consultant to the Child Care Health Team, a role I had served during most of my tenure at the health department.

"Well, it's good to see *you* again," I said.

It had been even better the night before when I'd had dinner with four friends I'd been in a women's group with. They'd planned the get-together after I'd written to them a few weeks earlier. In that letter I'd thanked them for their missives—post cards and letters crammed with news of work and families; a *Sweet Honey in the Rock* tape that I'd played before dawn at the bakery; tape-recorded segments of NPR's *Weekend Edition*. I wrote about how on days off, I'd crank up the espresso machine and listen to Scott Simon's warm voice and infectious laugh. When Bellingham weather reports and local news filled in the NPR program breaks, I could almost believe I was picking up radio reception. And in that letter, I'd admitted how much I missed them.

"You probably don't miss all of *this*," Carole said to me now, sweeping her arm around the office like a game show hostess presenting prizes to contestants. "There have been plenty of times the past few months I wished I could be in Stehekin along with you."

"How have things been?"

"Oh, it's pretty much the same old stuff. More and more work to do with fewer people. We've got a good team of supervisors, and everybody's working very hard."

Phones jangled in nearby offices. Mothers' voices soothed toddlers fussing in the immunization clinic waiting room. I surveyed the scene, so unchanged from when I'd been part of that supervisor team, and felt my heart beat a little faster. In earlier times, that would have been a sign of excitement. Today, it was the jab of failure that quickened my pulse.

"I must admit, I don't miss this stress," I said to Carole. "But I admire you for hanging in there. You're doing important work."

"Yeah, most of the time I feel that way." She glanced at her watch and then at her calendar. "Afraid I have to go to a meeting. We're gearing up for the flu clinics. Are you interested in coming back next month to give flu shots?"

"That might work," I said. "Let me know the schedule, and I'll try to plan my next consultation visit around that."

Two days later, any homesickness for Bellingham faded as I drove over Stevens Pass toward Stehekin.

Back in the Valley, rain pounded our metal roof the night before Halloween. Sometime while we slept, the temperature dropped, and we woke at six thirty to an inch of fresh snow. Just the day before, the kids had raked fallen maple leaves into a dome and jumped into the cushioning pile over and over until the day's sunshine faded. Now, the mound of red and gold was capped with white.

"Wow, look outside!" Matt hollered to anyone who was awake. Minutes later, he and Rachel bounded down the stairs in snowsuits and sweaters.

"Where are you going?" I asked.

"Out in the snow!" they both shouted.

"What about breakfast?"

"Later…"

"Not a bad way to start the day, is it?" I said to Jerry as I set granola and yogurt, juice, bowls, and glasses on the dining room table.

"Yeah, I'm just glad we don't have to get to work somewhere."

By the time the kids finished breakfast and bundled back up again for Jerry to take them to school, another inch-and-a-half of snow had accumulated.

I'd been recording our family experiences regularly on lined paper in a big, three-ring notebook. But that day, as snow folded in around the doors and windows, muffling the quiet into a deep silence, I sat at the dining room table with my own journal and entered into the broken, uncertain places in my heart. I wrote without thinking or censoring the questions that flowed through my pen. What had happened to my passion for public health? Where was the fervor that used to flush my cheeks when I presented in staff meetings about how childcare settings provided opportunities to promote health? Why had my zeal for immunizations, prenatal care, and serving the underserved disappeared? Just like on that hike to Goode Ridge with Jerry, I'd been trudging along in my work for years, one foot in front of the other, gritting my teeth, not really taking pleasure in the path I was on.

Conflicting values about service to others and care for myself battled in my mind, too. Words I'd spoken countless times to mothers of young children, child care providers, and other caregivers about the importance of self-care spilled onto the page, addressed to me. A reminder from Quaker writer Elise Boulding not to "outrun my guide" also made its way into my journal, surrounded by fear I would never again serve joyfully. How could my clarity about being called to nursing have gotten so blurred?

Fat snowflakes floated past the windows, settling on the growing mounds in the front yard. The wind blew some of the powder onto the front porch. In my previous life, such assertiveness by nature would have created havoc. Here, I followed the rhythm of feeding the woodstove and lighting candles and kerosene lamps between the electricity shutdowns. I timed my use of water and opening the refrigerator for the minutes the power returned. Someday I might curse this inconvenience, but today, the forced, slowed pace was a gift.

Jerry spent most of the day shoveling after each accumulation of snow covered the sidewalk and driveway. The hum of the refrigerator signaled we had power again just as I heard Jerry on the back porch stomping snow off his boots.

"I better put chains on the Suburban," he said. "We've got four inches of snow now, and I haven't seen Cragg come down this way yet with the plow. I'll go pick up the kids and see if there's any word about the Halloween party tomorrow night."

By the time Jerry and the kids returned, the layer of white measured six-and-a-half inches and was still growing. In Bellingham, a few inches of snow would shut down the entire town—no school, no buses, no concerts or meetings. But in Stehekin, it would take much more than half a foot of the stuff to cancel any of those. Cragg had plowed the roads, and the "Pumpkin Jubilee at the Gross Golden West" was still on.

Earlier in the week, a rummage through closets and dresser drawers, along with a trip to the Platform—Stehekin's version of a recycling center—had provided everything we needed for costumes. Jerry's pirate attire included a bandana, a black eye patch, and a homemade sword. Matt wore extra-large jeans held up with suspenders, an over-sized raincoat, and a red, plastic fireman's hat. He added to his clown look with a rouged nose and cheeks. Rachel spun around in a black turtleneck and skirt covered with orange felt pumpkins. She posed for a picture holding her entry in the Black-and-Orange-Dessert Contest—a two-layer carrot cake iced with orange cream cheese and decorated to look like a jack-o-lantern. I put on a purple T-shirt and green pants. When we arrived at the Golden West, I headed for the bathroom with a garbage bag stuffed with purple balloons. With Rachel's help and a package of safety pins, I emerged looking somewhat like a bunch of grapes.

Stehekinites of all ages streamed into the main room of the center. Jonathan and his friend Bob, a former Army Ranger, appeared in evening gowns, wigs, and earrings, their lips bright red and eyelids shimmering blue. Jean, as "Mrs. Frizzle the Grammar Expert," wore reading glasses on the tip of her nose and a ruffled blouse buttoned tight at her throat. There were ballerinas, Zorro, a robot, and an elf, too.

The big attraction for the kids was the games. At the Doughnut Dangle, Rachel and Matt lunged forward, hands clasped behind their backs, their mouths snapping and biting for powdered sugar doughnuts dangling on strings. Jerry and Ron dueled to stuff the most marshmallows into their mouths and still be able to mumble the words "flubby pumpkin." Jerry's cheeks bulged with ten marshmallows, but Ron, costumed as an overweight, nerdy couch potato sitting in a lawn chair, won with fifteen. Rachel's cake took first prize.

Stars lit the road, and the crunch of the Suburban's tires over the compact snow was the only sound as we headed home. "What did you guys think of the party?" Jerry asked.

"Cool," said Matt.

"Way more fun than trick-or-treating," Rachel said.

*   *   *

OVER THE NEXT FEW WEEKS, winter continued to flirt with the last days of autumn. The Halloween snowfall remained for days, then melted into the river as temperatures rose and precipitation came in the form of rain. Then, the thermometer would dip, swollen clouds would appear, and snow clumped on river rock and garden beds. Soon all the maples were bare, fir branches were tipped in white, and the road became a tunnel of plowed snow.

The number of hours of daylight shortened, adding to the quickened pace of preparations to host friends for Thanksgiving in Stehekin. Over the previous five years we'd built a tradition of sharing the Thanksgiving weekend with two Seattle-area families, the Evergreens and the Amber-Olivers. This year, John and Susan Amber-Oliver and their two boys couldn't come, but the Evergreens had committed to making the journey to Stehekin. Here, there would be no last minute phone calls about the menu and no Thanksgiving Day runs to Ennen's Market for missing ingredients. I'd consulted with other Stehekinites about how early to order a turkey and had checked and re-checked our pantry before mailing our grocery list to Safeway the week before the big day. We wanted the Evergreens to get a real Stehekin experience, just as long as it didn't include snow closing Stevens Pass, Safeway losing our grocery order, or The Lady breaking down. Over the course of our long friendship we'd shared so much, whatever the visit brought, it likely would just deepen our bonds.

*   *   *

ONE SUNDAY SOON AFTER WE HAD STARTED ATTENDING University Friends Meeting in Seattle, Sybil, a long-time attender, had told us after worship, "I think you should meet the Evergreens. Why don't you all come for tea at my apartment this afternoon?"

A few hours later, the two Jerrys, DeeDee, six-month-old Nick, and I (seven months pregnant) got acquainted under the satisfied gaze of Sybil, looking the part of a Jewish matchmaker seeking the perfect mate for a spinster daughter. She was right; we hit it off immediately. I'm sure none of us could reconstruct what we talked about that day, but I'm certain there was plenty of laughter, shared disdain for the Reagan administration, and admiration of Jerry and DeeDee's chubby, blue-eyed, wavy-haired baby boy.

Our friendship cemented firmly after Rachel and Matt were born and we began to share meals together every week or so. DeeDee and I met one morning a week with other new mothers from the Quaker community, and nearly every Monday night during football season, Jerry and I would bundle up the kids and arrive at the Evergreen house in time for the two dads to watch the game on television. Just before kick-off, DeeDee and I would nurse our babies; she'd then leave to sing with a group of friends, and I would go to a water exercise class.

The kids always seemed quite content when DeeDee and I returned, though we never were sure how much the dads attended to them during the game. Both men were avid football fans, and though DeeDee and I knew the kids were safe in their care, we suspected the babies' needs had to wait for time-outs. By the end of the season, Nick was walking, and Rachel and Matt were making their way around the living room on their hands and knees.

One evening, DeeDee and I returned to find trails of popcorn scattered across the living room floor. Jerry Evergreen, himself a twin, didn't so much walk as lurch due to cerebral palsy; Jerry Graville didn't have any excuse for not leaving the couch other than his intense focus on the game. We learned that the guys' strategy to entertain the kids was to toss popcorn varying distances and cheer them on as they crawled and toddled to snatch it.

Even after our move from Seattle to Bellingham, we'd checked in regularly about work, kids, Quaker meeting, politics, and how to make ends meet. We'd celebrated Jerry and DeeDee's adoption of three-year-old Jasmine when Nick was eight, and, a year later, Jerry Evergreen's decision to go to graduate school for a counseling degree. They had heartened me through the E. coli outbreak and had encouraged us when we decided to move to Stehekin.

*   *   *

"I hope we still have lots of snow when Nick's here," Matt said. "We can have some awesome snowball fights." Although Nick was only six months older than Rachel and Matt, he was nearing the end of middle school and had looked much more like an adolescent than a little boy when he'd visited in August. I worried he might find Stehekin boring, though as shy and reserved as he was, we'd likely never know it.

The Evergreens arrived the day before Thanksgiving, having made it safely over a snowy Stevens Pass in time to get on *The Lady* at Fields Point. As delighted as I was to see them tromp off the boat, I was equally glad to watch the crew unload our four boxes of groceries bulging with many of the ingredients for our holiday feast.

The next afternoon, the dining room table nearly sagged under the weight of a golden, twenty-pound turkey, DeeDee's legendary mashed potatoes, cranberry sauce, dressing and gravy, and my childhood family's tradition of mashed turnips and carrots (with lots of butter and a pinch of sugar). After pumpkin pie with whipped cream, as the sun started to slide down toward the peaks of McGregor, the kids went outside to play. While the boys built a snow fortress and piled up snowy ammunition, Rachel helped Jasmine make her first snowman.

We four adults sprawled in the warmth of the living room, a fire crackling in the barrel stove, and endorphins coursing through our bodies. Just like in previous years, we settled in for our traditional hashing over world affairs, jobs, and family. This time, though, I noticed that I wasn't grousing about the latest cutbacks at the health department or state and federal policies undermining public health. Those worries and stresses no longer occupied my mind. Instead, I talked about my fantasies, up until then only shared in a few conversations with Jerry, about writing and someday running a retreat center.

Earlier in the month I'd heard about a vacant house a few miles downlake. In my journal, I speculated about costs to house and feed people who wanted time in the wilderness to renew their bodies, minds, and spirits. I jotted names of organizations—Quaker and others—that might help fund such an endeavor. Although the asking price for the property didn't snuff my dreams of a hermitage on the lake, my journal pages still held unrelenting questions about whether God would really be satisfied if I served the world as a writer and retreat leader. That Thanksgiving, Jerry Evergreen added a different voice to the chorus of challenging ones I carried in my head.

"I have lots of therapist friends who'll come to your hideaway," Jerry said. "In fact, my entire agency should plan a week there."

"It seems kind of crazy to think I could pull it off," I said. "They're asking a million bucks for the house. Then there's all the other costs to run it as a business."

"Pffft," Jerry said, "million schmillion. You've never let a little thing like money stop you from going after something you want. You figured out how to support yourselves here, right?"

Perhaps I was being called to work that would feed my creativity as well as my desire to serve. Maybe my dreams weren't so crazy.

By the time the Evergreens were packing up on Sunday morning, Nick and Matt had schemed a plan for Nick and another friend to return on their own again in August, and the adults were thinking ahead to a repeat Thanksgiving celebration the next year.

"Good-bye, Mr. Snowman," Jasmine hollered as everyone piled into Colonel Mustard for the drive to *The Lady.*

CHAPTER 12

Stehekin Christmas

"Roof-alanche!" Matt shouted as a slab of snow slid off the steep metal roof and thumped to the ground, creating a wall outside one of our living room windows.

"That's what Mr. Scutt called it when the same thing happened at school the other day," Rachel said.

For days we'd watched the layer of white that glazed the rooftop like cake icing grow deeper. Temperatures had seesawed between the single digits and the low teens and then crept up to the thirties, turning the snow into a wet, leaden coating. Now, with the window blocked by a curtain of white, our place looked like the Alaskan Eskimo houses Rachel had studied for her "Living Environment" assignment at school. Matt and Jerry bundled up in snow pants, boots, gloves, down vests, and hats and went to work digging out the snow. When daylight once again streamed through the window, Rachel joined them outside, all three of them piling snow into a dome shape to construct their version of an igloo.

We'd decided to make most of our Christmas gifts, both out of necessity (no malls in Stehekin) as well as a desire to simplify and personalize our presents. I sewed quilts and potholders. Rachel and I used our new skill carving linoleum blocks to create a dozen images that I printed and bound into calendars. Matt knitted hats and whittled miniature, wooden black bears and cougars. Jerry sanded and glued dowels and bases for the wooden "Stehekin Slicer" bagel holder I'd designed. Stehekin might have insulated us from the Christmas shopping frenzy I'd witnessed when I was downlake, but just like everyone else, we were counting down the hours to the holidays. This year we had to factor in mail delivery only three days a week; we scrambled to get everything finished, wrapped, and mailed to my mom and Steve in California.

The morning Jerry left to drop the kids at school and take Mom and Steve's packages to the post office, my goal was to stash away our present-making supplies and find the shoebox of Christmas ornaments we'd included in our barge-load of household goods from Bellingham. As I searched through the closet in Matt's room, I found a box labeled Iris—Writing and Art. I dug under a bundle of rubber-banded pens, a rectangular tin of drawing pencils, and a Student Set of watercolors until I found Julia Cameron's book, *The Artist's Way: A Spiritual Path to Higher Creativity*, and under that, a hard-cover journal filled with one hundred blank pages.

Before our move, I'd worried that without work to direct my

hours in the winter, I'd spend my days watching videos, reading pulp fiction, and playing solitaire. A friend had recommended *The Artist's Way*, an outgrowth of Cameron's belief that creativity is a spiritual path, as a tool to give me a structure to explore writing, music, and painting. Scanning the Table of Contents now, I questioned if this book was for me. It was organized into weeks, twelve of them, and each chapter title started with the word *Recovering*. Would this be like a Twelve Step program? Some of the section headings added to my skepticism: "Your Ally Within;" "Affirmative Weapons;" "Poisonous Playmates;" "Finding the River;" "The Ivory Power;" and "Building Your Artist's Altar."

Other titles resonated, though: "Synchronicity;" "Perfectionism;" "Risk;" "Fear;" "Workaholism;" "Mystery." I flipped through to page ten, "The Basic Tools," and read about "morning pages"— three pages of longhand, stream-of-consciousness writing. I wasn't sure I was ready to tackle Cameron's exercises, and I'd always felt too hurried to journal. But now, with no job to report to every day, maybe this simple morning assignment was a place to start. I read Cameron's most important instruction—"There is no wrong way to do morning pages"—and placed the journal on my nightstand. The next morning, I made my first entry.

The week before Christmas, as I jotted the date for my morning write, I noted it as the anniversary eighteen years earlier of the death of my stepfather. I once again grieved the premature loss of this man who had buffered my mom's criticism of me, like that night before I headed off to nursing school nearly twenty-five years earlier. I imagined Dad approving of our decision to move to Stehekin and longed for his presence.

If morning pages were going to propel me into painful memories and self-examination, maybe the other chapters in *The Artist's Way* would offer a safety net—after the holidays.

*   *   *

THE SAME FLUCTUATING TEMPERATURES THAT HAD caused the roof-alanche earlier in the month challenged our hunt for a pine to cut for our Christmas tree. I thought back to years when the kids were little, squeezing between rows of stacked, compressed Douglas firs, blue spruces, and white pines in the lot at Seattle's "Chubby and Tubby's" hardware store on four-lane Aurora Avenue. This year, a hike through pristine, unplowed snow in a mountain valley just minutes from our home sounded blissful.

My vision of the tree search derived from watching too many Walt Disney films and episodes of *Little House on the Prairie* rather than the reality of propelling our knees and thighs through a mile of three-foot snow drifts coated with a layer of ice, the winter air chapping our cheeks. Sweat seeped from under my wool cap as I huffed to the first tree I came to.

"How about this one, guys?"

Jerry and the kids trudged yards ahead of me, pausing at a tree, rejecting it, and moving on to another.

"No," Jerry shouted back over his shoulder, "I see some better ones up ahead."

"But what's wrong with this one?" I called out.

"Over here," Matt said.

Just as I caught up with the three of them, I heard Jerry say, "It's pretty, but I think it's too big for the living room. Let's keep looking."

"What about the one we just passed?" Rachel asked. "It was nice and round." Her rosy cheeks were coated with sweat, and every time she took a step I could see the marks of melted snow on her pants.

"Let's just go a little further," Jerry said. "I like trees that aren't so bushy. It looks like there are some good ones not too far ahead."

"Just remember, once we cut it, we have to haul it out," I said.

"Dad, I'm getting tired," Matt said.

"Come on," Jerry said, "where's your sense of adventure?"

"Da-a-ad," the kids said in unison.

"Okay, okay. How about this one?"

"Great!" I shouted.

"Perfect," said Rachel as Jerry took the first swing with his axe.

The trudge back to the Suburban was slower going than the way in as we jockeyed for handholds on the tree trunk and dragged it over the snow. "I never realized we had such different preferences for Christmas trees," I said. "This one's pretty, but I think I would have been just as happy with the one we saw when we first got here."

"But that wouldn't have made nearly as good a story, would it?" Jerry said.

Later, revived by warm showers, dry clothes, and mugs of steaming hot chocolate topped with whipped cream, we adorned our fresh tree with the ornaments and a string of lights I'd pulled out of storage. Finally, I was able to take in the splendor of the day and the satisfaction of the hard work we'd shared.

The next morning, Matt and I woke up before Rachel and Jerry to find another foot of fresh snow. I hadn't imagined the quiet could become even quieter, but all sounds were muffled as gray clouds continued to dump fresh powder. I lit candles,

Matt turned on the Christmas tree lights, and we slid a CD of Christmas music into the boom box. This was exactly what I'd hoped for in this season usually frantic with buying and consuming. I expected the mood would change when Jerry's family arrived in a few days, but in the stillness of the morning, I savored the tranquility. Soon, the entire household was awake, and Jerry fired up the Suburban to drive the kids to school for their last day before the winter break.

Even though the cold and snow seemed to make the stars more brilliant, the sun brighter, the trees taller, and the mountains even more majestic than usual, five feet of snow on the ground and ice dangling from tree branches brought challenges that helped answer summer tourists' most common question—what do you do all winter? One morning, after stripping the beds and carrying an overflowing laundry basket to the unheated outbuilding behind the house, I found icy slush in the bottom of the washing machine. Another day, when I couldn't get the gas range to ignite, Jerry discovered ice blocking the air vent on the propane tank and spent the rest of the day thawing it out so we could cook. And though we'd mastered the Stehekin way of buying groceries, the decrease of boat runs to only five days a week required adjustments to menu planning and food ordering.

Driving the kids to and from school in the winter took extra planning, too. Colonel Mustard, with its heavy chassis and snow chains that looked like they were designed for an eighteen-wheel semi, was proving to be much more snow-worthy than Sir Arthur. The feminist in me felt only slightly guilty as I watched Jerry on his hands and knees in the frigid morning air, his chapped fingers cinching the chains around the Suburban's tires. We had discovered with the first few snowfalls that our end of the valley tended to get more snow than the head of the lake just six miles away, and Cragg didn't plow Company Creek Road until after the Stehekin Road was cleared. Though the Suburban needed the traction of chains to get the kids to school in the morning, it was likely Jerry would be back on his knees taking them off before picking up the kids in the afternoon.

Jerry had returned from that morning's school run to find me at the dining room table, sipping a cup of mint tea and finishing the grocery list I needed to get in that day's mail. Although we kept a good supply of staples on hand, this order included a ham and potatoes for our Christmas dinner plus extra eggs, milk, juice, ice cream, beer, and wine for our holiday guests—Jerry's parents, his sister Donna and her husband and thirteen-year-old daughter, and his cousin and her husband. As Jerry sat down with his own steaming mug, the lights started to flicker, a more common occurrence since the first snow at the end of October had knocked out the hydroelectric plant for several hours. Since then, we'd had shorter power outages during heavy-use times (often just around dinner) and when wet snow weighed down power lines.

"I wonder how your family will do if we lose power while they're here," I said. "Especially the ones from Portland and Seattle. They're pretty used to everything running without glitches."

"They're all outdoors-y types. They'll probably just think of it as part of the intrigue of spending Christmas in Stehekin," Jerry said. As if on cue, the CD stopped mid-carol, the refrigerator quit humming, and the lights went out.

Jerry and I looked at each other and chuckled. "I'm not sure your mom and sister will like the intrigue of not having running water if we lose power to the pump house and can't flush toilets or take showers," I said, lighting the candle we always kept on the table.

The following Wednesday, we experienced one of the "laws" of living in a ferry-served community—if boat mechanical problems are going to happen, they'll occur on the busiest travel days of the year. The day that family and groceries were to arrive, the winter boat—*The Lady Express*—broke down. That meant that *The Lady* (also affectionately known as "the slow boat") was brought out of hibernation to make the run with freight and visitors. Three hours after the scheduled arrival, *The Lady* delivered our holiday guests and most of our holiday food; the frozen items remained downlake on *The Lady Express* and came up on the repaired boat on Christmas Eve, three days later.

Stehekin's glistening winter splendor eclipsed the boat's delay, even for Dale, my hard-driving, investment banker brother-in-law. Everyone eased into the slower pace of uplake life as Jerry's folks and our niece, Leslie, settled in with us at our house, and the other four adults shared a cabin, with a hot tub, at the Silver Bay Inn at the head of the lake.

We filled the next few days with cross-country skiing, baking, and Hearts, the card game we always played at family gatherings. On Christmas Eve night, we all gathered at our house to read the story of Christ's birth, share blessings, and sing songs by candlelight. While logs crackled in the woodstove and snow again started to fall, we concluded the evening with another tradition instituted years earlier by Donna and Dale. One by one, each family member dumped little wrapped packages out of hand-made stockings; the rule was every item had to cost less than a dollar and had to fit in the sock. As always, laughter filled the room as everyone discovered miniature bottles of shampoo and French soaps lifted from hotel rooms, pens and note pads from pharmaceutical companies our pediatrician cousin picked up at medical conferences, individually-wrapped fruit leathers and chocolates, and an assortment of kitchen gadgets including a wide variety of closures for snack bags.

Matt, Rachel, and Leslie were well past the age of believing in Santa Claus, but waking to eighteen inches of fresh snow on Christmas morning was just as magical. Its powdery whiteness brightened the pre-sunrise hours as we opened more gifts, sipped lattés and hot chocolate, and ate orange twists and an egg-and-sausage casserole.

"Okay, guys," Dale said, pushing his chair back from the dining room table. "Time to get out in the snow!"

"Yeah!" the three teens agreed, dashing up the stairs to get into snow pants and sweaters.

"I guess the dishes can wait," I said. "We could ski to Boris' Bluff before we need to put dinner in the oven."

"Where's Boris' Bluff?" asked Windsor.

"It's a sweet spot in the woods behind the house here," Jerry said. "Boris goes back there with us on walks and climbs on the rocks."

"Sounds great!" Windsor said.

As Jerry's mom and I set dirty dishes in the sink, I noticed her cock her head toward Jerry and Windsor's conversation.

"Do you think Windsor can handle skiing?" I whispered.

"I don't know," she said. "He's not as strong as he used to be. But I know he'll want to try."

In October, Windsor's growing fatigue had sent him to the doctor; the non-Hodgkin's lymphoma he'd been diagnosed with two years earlier had returned. Except for the weakness Florence was concerned about, the second round of chemotherapy hadn't seemed to diminish the sparkle in Windsor's blue eyes or his enthusiasm for outings.

Cross-country skiing through the foot-and-a-half of fresh snow proved to be a workout for all of us. Windsor and Florence brought up the rear as the rest of us took turns breaking the trail through the woods. When the ground was bare, Boris the tabby cat and I could hike to his favorite spot in about twenty minutes; today the trek took close to an hour.

"This would be a great spot for a group photo," the pediatrician cousin said. He was an avid photographer and had packed in his 35 mm camera and tripod. "Everybody, climb up on top of Boris' Bluff!"

The moss-covered outcropping was mounded now with snow. Boris hadn't followed us there this time, but Murphy zigzagged through the snow and herded us all up the gentle slope. Windsor trudged his way toward the top as his wife, grandkids, and son, daughter, niece, and their spouses scrambled up the hill. He covered the last few feet on his hands and knees, and with a triumphant smile, he stood and posed behind his clan. Jerry slid an arm over my shoulders as I looked into his red-rimmed eyes.

Typically, we would have called my mom early on Christmas morning to wish her and Steve a happy holiday and to thank them for gifts. This year's call was postponed until after our return to the house to put the ham and scalloped potatoes in the oven. Florence and Donna offered to finish dinner preparations while Jerry, the kids, and I drove to the landing to make the call. We four huddled around the satellite phone in the little shelter near the post office as I punched in the numbers to Mom and Steve's place.

"Merry Christmas," we shouted in unison when I nodded my head that Mom was on the line.

A few seconds later, her voice reached over the delay with a greeting back. Then we heard the click of the extension phone, followed by Steve's voice.

"Hope you're warm down there," I said. "We woke up this morning to a foot-and-a-half of fresh snow." I rushed into the next sentence because any pause would be further delayed. "Jerry, the kids, and I are all standing around the phone and just wanted you to know we appreciate the gifts and money you sent." I paused for my words to reach her and for her voice to circuit back.

"You're welcome," she said. "Sorry we didn't send more, but we didn't know what to get you for out there, and we figured you could always use some cash." The phone went quiet, and I wasn't sure if she was taking a drag on a cigarette or if her next words hadn't been picked up yet by the satellite. "Thank you…"

"Yeah, the cash…" I stopped, realizing she was still talking.

"What?"

"That's okay, go ahead. Remember there's a lag time between when you speak and when we hear you." I closed my eyes and willed myself to wait for her next words. Jerry hopped up and down to stay warm, and the kids formed snowballs in front of the phone booth.

"Huh? Oh, yeah. I started to say thank you for the pretty calendar and that quilt you sent. I like the way it folds up into a pillow."

"You're welcome. I had fun making it, and I thought it would come in handy when you go on car trips."

Mom cleared her throat, then said, "What are Florence and Windsor doing for Christmas? Are they in Junction City or with Jerry's sister in Portland?"

"Uh, well, they're all here," I said. "They came up on the boat a couple of days ago and will be here for Jerry's birthday." The silence when I finished lasted even longer than usual.

"Oh," my mom said quietly. "Well, we never would have even tried to drive up there. You can't ever tell what the weather will be like. I guess we're just not as gutsy as you guys and Florence and Windsor. We're just fine here with going to Cracker Barrel for their Christmas dinner special."

"I hope you'll come visit sometime," I said. "Maybe when the snow's all gone." I tapped on the phone booth window and motioned to the kids to come over. "The kids…"

"Well, we'll see. What? Did you say something? I thought you were done. I can't figure out the timing on that damn satellite phone. I'll shut up, now."

"Sorry, I know it's frustrating. I was just saying the kids want to say something. We're getting pretty cold out here, so I'll let them sign off. Merry Christmas to both of you."

I handed the receiver to Rachel. As she, and then Matt, chattered about school and the snow, I reached to Jerry for a hug. I knew that, in her way, my mom loved me and was proud of me, but her disapproval of my life choices traversed the satellite delay louder than words. Maybe the Stehekin credo of "not getting along is not an option" would teach me some better ways to listen to her, to reach out to her as my mother, without being flattened by her critical voice.

After dinner a couple of nights later, we all again lounged around the cabin. Dale, who just days earlier had been pushing us to plan and go and do, sat contemplatively on the couch with a pencil and yellow legal pad. A year before we moved to Stehekin, he'd been diagnosed with metastatic prostate cancer.

Remarkably, he'd responded well to surgery and chemotherapy and seemed to go into remission quickly. Although Dale maintained his usual drive at work, he'd become more devout in his evangelical Christian faith and more reflective through writing poetry. That night, he read aloud a poem he'd been writing and revising over the previous couple of days. Stehekin was working its magic on Dale, too.

A few minutes later, the refrigerator's hum clunked.

"What happened?" Donna asked.

"Power went out," Matt said.

"We wanted you to have the full Stehekin experience," Jerry said. "It'll probably come back on as soon as our neighbor, Karl, drives down to the power station and figures out what the problem is. It could be awhile, though, so we might as well call it a night."

The Silver Bay contingent bundled up to return to the cabins at the head of the lake. We equipped Florence, Windsor, and the kids with flashlights as they started upstairs for bed, and Jerry and I went to work on the last bit of cleanup by the light of kerosene lamps.

"How do you think your dad's doing?" I asked Jerry as he scrubbed a baking pan. He let the scouring pad float in the sink and leaned back on the counter.

"Man, I don't know. I never thought I'd see him crawl through the snow."

"Shocked me, too," I said, as I slid my arms around Jerry's waist. "We should ask your mom when his next check-up is."

The next morning, still without electricity, Jerry walked down to Karl's house for an update. When everyone arrived for breakfast, they found us transferring the contents of the fridge into snow-filled ice chests on the front porch. Jerry reported that a blown transformer had caused this power outage; with the holidays, it probably wouldn't be fixed for a couple of days.

"We've got plenty of wood for the stove, so we'll be warm, and the cook stove runs on propane, so we can cook and bake," he said.

"That means we can still make your birthday cake," Rachel said.

"The bad news is," Jerry went on, "without electricity, we don't have a pump, which means we don't have water."

"No water for coffee?" Donna said.

"We can haul water from the river and use that for drinking," Jerry said. "And we can melt snow on the stove to use to flush the toilet, but we won't be able to shower."

"I'm sure glad I showered and washed my hair yesterday morning," Donna said. "As long as I can make coffee, I'll be okay."

And we were all okay, enjoying the snow and the quiet and the camaraderie that pervades times of challenge. After dinner that night, we all cheered as Jerry blew out the forty-two candles on his chocolate-zucchini birthday cake.

By the third day of the power shutdown, though, as our visitors were packing up to head home, the entire valley seemed to be feeling the strain of hampered hospitality. Word spread quickly that the Lodge had fired up its generator and was offering showers and fresh-brewed coffee by donation. Donna was the first of our crew to get in line with her travel mug, towel, and clean clothes. I was right behind her.

CHAPTER 13

Spirit at Work

Once the new year began, we resumed our Stehekin winter schedule. We rose around seven, ate breakfast, and drove the kids to school. After kitchen cleanup, the sun just edging above McGregor, Murphy and I tromped through the snow. Some mornings we had to break a trail through a fresh buildup of snowfall; other days we practically skated down Company Creek Road, its snowy cover compressed to an icy glaze by Cragg's plow. After the day's walk, I returned home to long stretches of solitude.

While Jerry worked on endless winter tasks—shoveling snow; splitting and stacking firewood and hauling it into the house; keeping the truck and the Suburban running—I delved more deeply into my frustration about work as a nurse, my yearning for a more creative life, and my desire to hear and respond to what God called me to.

As Julia Cameron instructed, most mornings I closed the bedroom door, leaned against the bed's headboard with my journal propped on my knees, and filled three pages. Typically, I scrawled questions. *Is it possible that this leading of the past twenty years is over? Are my feelings of burnout a signal I'm called to a new path? Have I stayed in nursing because it serves my own need to feel valued rather than out of compassion for those I care for? If I follow my heart's desire to write, am I turning my back on those in need? What am I supposed to do with my life?*

One day in mid-January, I received a letter inviting me to join the roster of health reviewers for Head Start programs. I'd be part of a team sent to spend a week in a program, so it didn't matter where I lived; I just had to get myself (at the Federal government's expense) to the Head Start center being reviewed. I wasn't sure that I wanted to re-enter the public health world, but I couldn't deny that the few glowing embers of my former fire for nursing sparked. I readied my reply of acceptance for the next mail day.

My first review was for a program in Wenatchee, just an hour from the downlake parking lot at Fields Point where we left the Tempo. Although I didn't have to venture far, I knew I'd be in a different world from my Stehekin way of life. Packing my suitcase for the week, I reached deep into the closet, bypassing jeans and sweat pants for a couple pairs of crisply creased dress slacks. I dug to the bottom of dresser drawers, underneath long underwear and bulky sweaters, for turtlenecks and cardigans. I left my Sorel snow boots in the mudroom and polished the black clogs I hadn't worn for months.

Determined to maintain my practice of morning pages, I slid my spiral-bound journal and a wooden pen, hand-turned by Don Pitts, into my canvas briefcase.

Ever since I'd gone to work for the state health department when Rachel and Matt were four, and up until I quit at the county health department, periodic business trips took me away from home for three to ten days at a time. I enjoyed those respites from parenting and knew that the kids, and Jerry, were skillful at managing in my absence. In fact, I suspected that they all enjoyed letting some chores slide, eating a few extra pizza meals, and staying up later. I also knew that the income from this work would help stretch our finances during the winter. What I hadn't expected was the surge of excitement I felt reading the pre-review materials the team leader had sent and thinking about sharing my expertise in children's health.

At the first meeting of the review team, we went around the table introducing ourselves. As each of the other members ticked off titles with various Head Start programs or credentials as specialists in early childhood education, my mouth went dry. A few years earlier, I would have identified myself as a child-care nurse consultant for the state health department, or as the chair of the statewide Child Care Coordinating Committee and a contributor to the Child Care Health Performance Standards of the American Public Health Association. Had I been on this team just the year before, I would have been there as a communicable disease supervisor of a county health department. That day, though, I stuttered through my introduction. I couldn't say I was on staff anywhere, but I wasn't ready to identify myself as a former nurse—or as a part-time baker. Instead, I mumbled something about being on a sabbatical and looking forward to applying my experience in a new role.

Over the next five days, I found I enjoyed getting to know the team members and program staff and learning from their perspectives as early childhood educators, administrators, and mental health and developmental specialists. The Head Start classrooms delighted me as I observed skilled teachers nurture energetic four- year-olds, while at the same time teaching them to wash their hands and sample new foods.

The dawn-to-dark work schedule, though, allowed little time for the quiet reflection that had become part of my daily routine at home. I was exhausted from the early morning arrivals at sites; hours of observing in classrooms, interviewing parents and staff and reviewing policies and records; and late-night meetings with team members to coalesce our varied perceptions into a report of the program's strengths and areas needing improvement.

It wasn't only the review routine that drained my energy, though. For the first time since our move, I had access to cable television and a telephone. As the days went on and I became more overwhelmed by the amount of information to process, I succumbed to the mindless escape the television offered. Too many nights I clicked through the numbers on the remote control, hoping to find an episode of *Friends, Northern Exposure,* or *The West Wing.*

The telephone in my hotel room beckoned me, too. In Stehekin, the satellite phone in the cement-floored, closet-like enclosure at the landing was a tool we used only in emergencies. A phone chat with my friend, Pat, from the warmth and comfort of my bed, was a rare treat. Bolstered by that one, I decided to give my mom a call. I knew that one of the most distressing aspects for her of our move to Stehekin was that she couldn't reach us by phone. Hearing my voice would be a gift to her.

As usual, Steve answered. "I'll get your mom," he said, immediately handing me off to her, as if every minute he talked to me was a theft from my mom.

"Where are you?" were the first words she spoke. "Is everything ok?"

"Yes, everything's fine. I'm downlake on a Head Start review. They put us up in a hotel, so I have a phone."

"Oh, it's so good to hear your voice." I detected the quiver of tears in hers. "I just hate not being able to talk to you guys."

"I know it's hard. That's why I wanted to call while I had access to a phone."

"So what's this Head Start thing you're doing? Do they pay you?"

"Yes, it's actually pretty good pay." I fiddled with the TV remote, my index finger hovering over the on button. "I'm here all week with a team of people reviewing the program. We'll write a report about things they're doing well and things they need to improve on. I'm enjoying the work, but I don't like being away from home."

"I'm glad to hear you're getting paid. I worry about how you guys are making it financially. I still can't believe you quit a good job to go there."

"Lots of my co-workers said they think we're courageous."

"Well, seems kind of irresponsible to me."

I swung my legs over the edge of the bed, stood up, and paced as far as the phone cord let me, clamping my mouth to block a defensive reply. How had she known I'd passed that same judgment on myself as I'd watched the Head Start staff at work?

"Don't worry, Mom. We're really doing fine financially. And this job adds a nice little cushion until Jerry and I go back to work in the summer. I'm just glad I don't have to do it every day."

"Do what? Nursing?"

"Yeah, I'm pretty burned out. Other people might think it took courage to quit my job, but it was more like desperation for me," I said, repeating the belief I'd expressed to my former coworker in the fall. "I don't know that I'll go back to it."

"Sounds like you're having a mid-life crisis." I imagined a sneer curled around her words, and I felt like one of the pre-schoolers I'd been with all week.

"I don't think it's as much a crisis as an opportunity," I said after a couple more strides beside the bed. "I think maybe I'm supposed to be doing something different with my life."

"You're damn lucky to be able to just walk away from a good job while you try to figure out what to do with your life. I never had that luxury. Your dad and I had to do whatever work we could to pay the bills."

We'd entered the familiar terrain of questions and criticism from my mom and self-doubt for me. I didn't want to follow this trail again.

"You're right, I am lucky, and I'm grateful I have this chance to re-think my work and to have more time with the kids while they're young. It's turning out to be a good experience for them, too."

"Well, I'm glad for that."

I waited, hoping she'd ask more about her grandchildren and what they were doing in school. As the silence lengthened, I asked how she was doing.

"Oh, I've been sick as a dog," she said, ticking off symptoms I'd heard from her for years about her bowels, a funny taste in her mouth, tingling in her hands, and pain in her back and hips. "But I'll survive."

"Well, I hope you feel better soon," I said. "I should sign off now. I have a meeting early in the morning, and I know it's getting late for you, too."

"Okay, good to talk to you. Tell everybody I said hello." I heard a catch in her voice again. "I love you."

"Love you too, Mom. Good night."

I replaced the receiver in its cradle with more vigor than needed and reached for a Kleenex. Dammit, she'd done it again. Pushed on those tender spots of insecurity and longing for her approval. Her comments about mid-life crisis had hit an especially vulnerable place. Hadn't I scorned nurses who'd abandoned nursing mid-career? Wasn't I the one who'd mentally scoffed at a colleague when she left advocacy work to open a dress shop on the Oregon coast? I carried enough judgments about my disillusionment with nursing without any help from my mom.

As the week wore on, I missed the daily writing, meditation, and walking in the woods that had started to restore my sense of equilibrium. Being away from Jerry and the kids and missing out on the news of their lives untethered me. If this kind of consulting was how I'd serve the world in the future, I had much to learn about how to do it in a sustainable way.

By the time I boarded *The Lady* at Fields Point a few days later, I was more than ready to take off my nurse consultant hat and return to the solitude at the other end of the lake. In my hotel room, I'd skimmed enough bad comedy, sensational talk shows, and insulting commercials to convince me that the videotaped episodes of *ER* that Jerry's mom sent to us, plus the movie videos that people shared around the valley, were a fine alternative to TV reception. The conversation with my mom had left me relieved that telephone lines didn't reach our Stehekin home. And the hours in windowless conference rooms with our team of ten consultants scrutinizing three-ring binders full of plans, stacks of files, and reams of reports led me to question how the money spent on this review would help the children, families, and their Head Start caregivers.

Back in Stehekin after the Wenatchee review, I returned to my journal and the questions littering its pages. For the first time in my adult life, I was permitting myself to seriously consider different work and the possibility that nurturing my creativity might lead me to new and valid ways to serve God. Despite doubts that I had a single artistic bone, I returned to the structure of *The Artist's Way* to give shape to my exploration.

Like the straight-A high school student I'd been, I completed the book's assignments in listing "what I would try if it weren't too crazy." Even though I scorned some of Cameron's exercises, I scrawled my own crazy ideas: create a hermitage for people to retreat to, travel to France and Italy, spend a year at Pendle Hill Quaker Center in Philadelphia, and never again work as a nurse. The next list, "what I would do if it weren't so selfish," trailed down the page: spend more time alone, take a swing dance class, not work at a paying job.

I continued to carve images of mountains and waterfalls onto linoleum blocks, roll black ink onto them, and make prints for cards. I invested in more colored pencils, watercolors, pastels, and drawing paper and opened myself to hue, texture, and form. I dusted off the flute I'd learned to play in third grade and filled it with my newly-deepened breath and the aching of my heart. And I wrote.

For years I'd admired and purchased countless hand-bound journals with creamy, deckle-edged, blank pages. I'd commit to writing each morning and would do just that for a week or two.

Gradually, my entries dwindled, my journaling time squeezed out by getting the kids ready for school, swimming laps at the Y, grabbing a latté and a scone to eat at my desk at the health department. That winter, though, I filled first one, then another, 100-page blank book.

Many of the pages held the same questions I'd taken with me to Wenatchee. Some days I had clear, positive answers, only to have the doubts reappear in similar form a few days or weeks later. Day after day, in the privacy of our mountain home, I peeled away layer upon layer of uncertainty about my work and my worth. I might be bundled in sweaters, wool socks, long underwear, gloves, and a down jacket when I took the kids to school or went to the landing for mail and groceries, but at home, in silent meditation and while writing those pages, I was as naked as Jerry had been on the trail to Goode Ridge. As the days grew shorter, the snow piled deeper, and the air chilled my skin on daily walks, I recognized the intensity of my exhaustion.

Finally, I admitted I was tired of taking care of others.

Now, "mid-life crisis" and "burnout" seemed to trivialize what was a bigger search for me, and, I discovered, for many people. One of the books I'd packed for Stehekin was *The Reinvention of Work: A New Vision of Livelihood for Our Time,* by theologian Matthew Fox. His assessment that the industrial revolution led to factory-oriented models and ideals of work resonated with my distress over health care system demands to quantify nursing care; the caring part seemed to hold little value.

I was coming to some new understandings of the place of work in my spiritual journey, too, when I read Fox's appraisal: "Work comes from inside out; work is the expression of our soul, our inner being. It is unique to the individual; it is creative. Work is an expression of the Spirit at work in the world through us."

Spirit at work in the world through us. That was how I'd once felt about nursing, but now I was unclear about how I could best serve the world. And I was moving toward new beliefs about that mystery, that presence, that I call God and about what that voice was guiding me to do. After days of sitting alone with my reading and my journal, I was looking forward to the distraction of friends coming to visit.

We'd met Nancy Ewert a few years earlier at a Quaker gathering. Our friendship grew as we visited her, her husband Greg, and their two daughters at their home on Lopez, one of Washington's San Juan Islands. We'd also been infected by Greg's love of juggling, and at his urging, Jerry and Matt had attended the annual Juggle Fest on Lopez in mid-September. For an entire weekend, they'd camped out with jugglers—novice to expert—from all over the Pacific Northwest. When I picked them up at the boat on their return, Matt talked nonstop about playing and practicing with balls, clubs, and cigar boxes. He didn't even blush when he told me about the festival's grand finale on Saturday night—naked jugglers tossing and passing flaming clubs.

In addition to the allure of Juggle Fest, Greg's enthusiasm about Lopez and its school, where he was a teacher, had contributed to our thoughts of the island, instead of Bellingham, as a potential home after Rachel and Matt finished eighth grade at Stehekin School. The Ewert family visit would be a time not only to introduce them to Stehekin, but to delve into the possibility of a future move to their island community.

After record snowfall the previous two months, we had high hopes of fresh powder for cross-country skiing and snowman-building with these friends from west of the Cascades. The San Juan Islands' marine climate and the rain shadow of the Olympic Mountains range lead to mild winters on Lopez.

Unfortunately, Stehekin's unique micro-climate conspired that weekend in mid-January, with the precipitation coming in the form of rain, not snow. We took refuge in an intricate snow cave one of our friends had built, the frigid Stehekin gurgling past a few feet away.

"This is cool," Greg crowed as his family and ours sipped hot chocolate in the cozy shelter. "You guys are so lucky to live in Stehekin."

"Yep, we are," I said. "I just wish we'd had some beautiful fresh snow for you guys instead of this slush."

"Hey, no need to apologize," Greg said. "This is way more snow than we ever get on Lopez."

Later that night, after all the kids were in bed, we four adults lingered over wine in the warmth of our living room.

"I think you guys would love it on Lopez," Greg said.

"We're giving it serious thought," Jerry said. "Just have to work out a few things, like jobs, housing… you know, little stuff like that."

"Man, after what you've done to be here, you'll figure it out on Lopez," Greg said. "And we'll help you."

"There's a lot that's appealing about the island," Jerry said picking up one of the juggling clubs Greg and the kids had been practicing with earlier. "Seems like it's got many of the things we love about Stehekin, plus some of what's missing, like a high school."

"But on a more manageable scale," I said. "I can't picture the kids going to a school in Bellingham with over a thousand students. A high school with just a hundred seems much better after their time in the little Stehekin School."

"It'd be great to have them at Lopez," Greg said as he pulled two more clubs from his duffel bag.

"Well, they're only halfway through seventh grade," I said. "We've got time to get clear about where we'll all go next." We fell into silence, watching Greg twirl all three clubs over his head.

CHAPTER 14

Mud Flats Season

"DID WE REALLY WISH FOR MORE snow back in January?" I asked the kids one morning at breakfast in mid-March. Four inches had drifted down overnight, and the power lines were sagging again. And once again, I filled the teakettle and bathtub with water and checked that candles and kerosene lamps were on the table and windowsills. This seemed to be its own season between the dark of winter and the blossom of spring—a season of gray slush and mud, offering then retracting the sun, bare ground, and new growth.

By the next day, though, what turned out to be the last snow of the winter had melted, leaving behind ridges of mud on the road's shoulder and potholes overflowing with water. The sun rose a little earlier that morning, and daylight didn't disappear until we sat down for dinner. Each day more of the garden fence appeared around the snow-covered beds; by the end of the week, enough snow had melted under the clothesline that I could hang laundry to dry outside. We started shedding wool gloves, hats, long underwear, and layers of sweaters and turtle-necks; most days we favored hiking shoes, not our wool-lined Sorels; and we let the woodstove's morning fire die out until we needed heat again as the sun slid behind the treeline about the time the kids got home from school.

One Sunday afternoon later that month, Jerry, the kids, and I piled into the Suburban with Murphy in the back. The further down-valley we drove, the smaller the snowy piles on the roadside that Cragg had cleared with his plow. Among the cluster of houses deep in the woods before the turn-off to Har-lequin Bridge we saw the last pine branches still tipped in snow. I rolled the window down partway as we rumbled across the bridge; the river below glistened and I knew it remained frigid, but the rush of air across my cheeks was warmer than I'd felt in months.

By the time we got to the head of the lake, the paved road was bare and dry. Old Subaru and Volvo wagons and an assort-ment of aged vans and pickups lined the shoulder at the cut-off to Silver Bay. Children's voices chirped, accompanied by the springtime song of the Western Tanager, and a bright blue kite dipped and swerved against the pale turquoise sky. Stehekin might not have phone service or a radio station, but somehow nearly everyone in the Valley (and surely all of the kids) seemed to know this was the opening day of "Mud Flats Season"—a short interval between the final melting of the snow and the raising of the level of Lake Chelan.

Every fall, the Chelan County Public Utility District low-
ers the lake about twenty feet to make room for spring runoff
from mountain snowpack. That water diversion leaves a large,
bare area at the head of the lake at Silver Bay, just beyond the
cabins where Jerry's family had stayed at Christmas. All winter,
the uplake water laps at the snowy shore. But once the temperatures start to warm in the spring, this stretch of land is the
first place to be clear of snow, and it turns into the closest thing
Stehekin has to a sandy beach.

"Hey, Matt and Rachel, come over here," Mugs called, as he
tossed a Frisbee to his dad, Jonathan. Their yellow lab, Mitt,
danced between them. Mugs' jeans were rolled up to his knees,
and muck coated his bare feet. Murphy got into the game before the kids did only because he didn't have to take off socks
and shoes.

Jerry and I slipped out of our rubber boots and socks, too,
and I squeegeed the cool glop between my toes. I breathed in
the spring air and scanned the scene: another kite dueling with
the first one we'd seen; kids crouched down to examine shreds
of cedar bark, driftwood, and rocks. I reached for Jerry's hand
as we traced the channels of water crisscrossing the sand, mim-
icking a river's flow.

"We have to bring Kevin and Lori here when they come
visit," Matt said half an hour later as we bundled back up and
headed toward the car. Even though the days were getting longer, the sun started to sink behind Devore Peak around four
thirty, and the breeze off the lake carried a bite.

The following Saturday, Jerry's older brother, Dick, his wife
Cathy, and their two children, Lori and Kevin, arrived from
Idaho. Cathy home-schooled the kids, who bracketed Matt

and Rachel in age, and the family had decided to spend a few days with us as a kind of spring break. On our way home from the landing, we stopped at the mud flats, then returned every afternoon after we picked up Rachel and Matt at school.

We wound up Dick's family's Stehekin visit with a two-mile hike to Buehler's Bluff, a spot known only to locals. The steep trail was a workout for the adults as well as the teenagers, but the reward was a raven's-eye view of the head of the lake, a floatplane gliding into the landing, Weaver Point, and glimpses of the Lakeshore Trail. From our vantage point at the top of the bluff, the mud flats looked like a National Geographic map of a desert in the Middle East. The lowering of the water level etched the earthy brown lake bottom with curving patterns of retreat.

"I could look at this view all day," Dick said.

"I never get tired of it either," I said, "but we did promise the kids we'd make pizza for dinner tonight. We should get going."

Although the hike down Buehler's Bluff was less of a challenge, everyone cheered when we got to the Stehekin Road; the kids sprinted to the Suburban waiting for us on the shoulder.

"What's on the windshield?" I said.

Jerry slid a rectangle of white paper from under the wiper blade on the driver's side and unfolded it. "It's a message from the Park office. I'm supposed to call my mom."

From the passenger's side, I looked across the top of the car to meet Jerry's eyes and caught a flicker of worry. Instead of heading up-valley, we did a U-turn and drove to the landing. While Jerry talked on the satellite phone, Dick, Cathy and I waited in the car; Rachel and Matt led their cousins to Mr. Scutt's bike stand to show them where Matt hoped to work that summer.

"Mom said Dad just had a physical and a CAT scan," Jerry told us after he hung up. "It wasn't good. The lymphoma has spread and they think he's only got six to eight weeks. Mom wants us all to come visit."

My thoughts shifted to Florence and Windsor's visit to Stehekin just three months earlier and Windsor's crawl through the snow to the top of Boris' Bluff for our group picture. In the weeks since then, the snow melted, trillium and Sitka columbine started to bloom, the mud flats lengthened, and I had shelved Windsor's failing health in the back of my mind. We'd made plans for a downlake trip, first to Bellingham to talk to our renters about the possibility of buying our house, then to Lopez to see the Ewerts and check out the high school. Now, with this news from Florence, we needed to head south first, to Junction City, to say good-bye.

*   *   *

"I'M SO GLAD YOU'RE HERE," Jerry's mom said a few days later as we all trooped into the house Jerry had grown up in; it had become like a second home to the kids and me over the past fifteen years. Matt and Rachel hauled their duffel bags to what used to be Jerry's room where, from the time they were two, they had stayed for a week every summer while Jerry and I vacationed in Stehekin.

"How's Dad?" Jerry asked his mom.

"Not so good. He's in bed. Only gets up to go to the bathroom, hardly eats anything. I know he'll be glad to see you, but he might not have much to say."

"How are *you* doing?" I asked Florence as Jerry headed toward the bedroom.

"Okay." Her chin crumpled, and her eyes reddened. "I'm trying to be strong."

"You *are* strong," I said, "and maybe we can give you some help."

Over the next few hours, Jerry, the kids, and I took turns sitting with Windsor. The kids told him about the "roof-alanches" and the snow cave Jerry had helped them build. Windsor would nod, close his eyes, the corners of his mouth arcing upward as if playing the scene in his mind. We gave him an update on Sir Arthur, assuring him his dad's truck had made it through its first winter in Stehekin. The stories about life in Stehekin seemed to stir his memories. Soon he was telling tales about his own years in a one-room schoolhouse.

In the following days, Windsor cycled through thoughts about the present and his youth, interspersed with times of restlessness and dozing. As I had experienced often in the nearly twenty years I'd known him, Windsor didn't reveal much about his feelings, but he did ask about what was happening to his body.

"I just don't understand why I'm so weak," he said one afternoon while I sat at his bedside. Jerry had convinced Florence to take a nap, and I was grateful for the break from her intensified efforts to anticipate everyone else's needs. Her mutterings under her breath about whether the kids were hungry, wondering if we needed to do our laundry, or fretting about what time we should have dinner drove me nuts. I wanted to be patient and understanding of her and just wished she'd let us take care of her for a change. At least Windsor seemed to recognize that I had some kind of expertise and ability to handle a difficult situation.

"Iris," Windsor asked again, "why do you think I don't have any energy?"

"Well, the lymphoma has affected your whole body, you know. It's putting all of its energy into fighting off those cancer cells."

"Sure has happened fast..." his voice faded and his eyelids slowly closed as he drifted off to sleep.

I held his hand and stroked his short, square fingertips. I looked at those hands that had been able to fix anything. I thought of all the changes he'd witnessed in his lifetime. I suspected he had strong feelings, disagreements, and concerns about many of those changes, yet his blue eyes typically lit up when he discovered something he didn't know about. Jerry had told me he felt disapproval from his dad when he was in college and in his early years after graduating. They never argued, but Jerry sensed his dad was disappointed he hadn't used his business degree and instead had worked in soup kitchens and taken care of alcoholics who lived on the streets. Any displeasure Windsor felt about Jerry's lifestyle, though, seemed long past by the time the two of them spent that week getting Sir Arthur running.

Even though Florence had confirmed that Windsor's doctor believed the lymphoma was advancing rapidly and would no longer respond to treatment, I was surprised how readily they accepted the services of hospice. Perhaps Windsor's increasing weakness and pain halted them from resisting the hospice nurse's visit the day after we called to request care. I was grateful to be there to be Windsor's advocate when the nurse arrived, but that role wasn't necessary. She was the kind of nurse I had strived to be when I worked with hospice ten years earlier, and I felt a twinge of longing for that role. She responded with the warmth of a close family member and the efficiency of a skilled caregiver as she secured a prescription

for pain medication and counseled Florence about how to keep
Windsor at home. By the next day, he was resting comfortably
in a hospital bed set up in his bedroom, cared for in shifts by
his wife and sons and daughter and their spouses.

Jerry and I had decided that he would stay in Junction City
while the kids and I went to Bellingham and Lopez for the rest
of their spring break. The night before we were to leave, we
held each other in bed.

"It's sad to think this may be the last time the kids and I
see your dad. I dread saying good-bye tomorrow," I whispered
through tears. I wanted to be more of a comfort to Jerry, but
my grief took over. He smoothed my hair off my forehead and
kissed it gently.

"Yeah, it's hard to think of you leaving, but I think it's important for the kids to have some fun on spring break."

"You're right, I know. But it's as if by staying here, staying
with him, I can hold him longer, keep him from dying. It's hard
to let him go."

Jerry nodded wordlessly, a small choke coming from his
throat. Just as his mom and brother had done that morning, he
started to cry. I wrapped my arms around him and held him as
we both cried ourselves to sleep.

The next week blurred like the roadsides along the interstate as I drove, with the kids, the three hundred miles from
Junction City to Bellingham, then south again an hour to
Anacortes for the ferry to Lopez. At least I could talk to Jerry
daily on the phone for updates about his dad, but I missed his
calm and optimistic presence as I worried about the future. We
didn't know yet where we'd live during the upcoming summer
season in Stehekin, and I'd already started to fret about how
we'd support ourselves if we moved to Lopez and whether we

could find affordable housing there. Not surprisingly, I came down with a nasty cold.

One attraction to Lopez for us was the presence of a small, Quaker worship group there. That Sunday of our visit, I sat in the silence of one family's mobile home and prayed my doubts about the future. After nearly nine months of practicing opening myself to God's will, I was feeling no more clear about what I was called to do than those first days when I traded in my public health nurse name tag for a baker's apron. Away from the security and rhythm of the Stehekin Valley, I asked for signs that we could, or should, continue to take our cues from Spirit rather than from others' expectations of how we should live. The strength of my trust seemed as fragile as the pine saplings that had started to poke through the soil charred by the previous summer's fire. That fire had loosened my grip on the desire to control, but my palms, now clasped in prayer, still sweat with fear of the unknown.

As the kids' spring break wound down, it was obvious that Windsor's death was near and that Jerry should remain in Junction City. Matt, Rachel, and I returned to Stehekin and tried to resume our usual activities. I trekked to the landing every day to call Jerry for updates. A few days after we got home, Jerry's weary voice stumbled as it bounced from his folks' house, to some circling satellite, to the phone in Stehekin.

"How's your dad doing today?" I asked.

The pause before his response was even longer than usual as I heard his brother's voice in the background.

"Honey, I have to go. I think this might be it. Call me tomorrow."

The next day, I listened as Jerry's words caught up with the delayed transmission to describe the scene the day before. Just after he'd heard my voice on the phone, his brother called to him from the living room. The two sons and Florence gathered around Windsor's bed as his breathing slowed and his body relaxed. Within a few minutes, he took his last breath.

"I'm so glad you were there," I choked.

"Yeah, me, too."

I waited, not knowing what else to say.

"The funeral is this weekend," Jerry said. "I know you just got home, but…"

"Of course, we'll be there. I wish it were easier to talk about everything right now, but we'll have time when we get there. We'll take the boat out tomorrow."

The Suburban sputtered as I headed toward home. Gray clouds hovered over the mud flats, smothering the hints of spring we'd had just a few weeks before. My heart ached for Florence, knowing she now faced all of her days alone. All I wanted was to be back in her warm kitchen with Jerry's arms holding my grief. Without him, the months of our rustic lifestyle felt worn and frayed. What had earlier seemed charming—ordering groceries and books by mail, improvising with car and house repairs, power outages, slush in the washing machine—now weighted me like the heavy winter boots I was ready to shove into the back of the closet.

CHAPTER 15

Not-so-Simple Lifestyle

EVEN THOUGH THE SPRINGTIME LIGHT AND BREEZE
leaked through the ill-fitting windows and doors, a rank
smell of animal droppings and pack rat permeated the air.

"Welcome to home, sweet home," Cragg said as he pushed
open the cabin's heavy wooden door.

It was mid-April, and everyone in Stehekin was gearing up
for summer's frenzy. Ever since our return to the valley after
Windsor's funeral, much of our attention had turned to finding housing for mid-June through August, the prime tourist
season. Our search had brought us to this cabin that Robbie
and Cragg owned.

"Don't worry," Cragg said, "once it's cleaned up, this'll be a
good place for you guys." I nodded silently and consoled myself

that the cabin was just five minutes from the bakery, and the rent was just seventy-five dollars a month. Cragg held the door open, waved Jerry and me in, and batted at a little swarm of mosquitoes circling our heads. "Watch your step, it drops down a bit to the kitchen."

The cobblestone floor caught my sandals and stubbed my bare toes. To my left, a porcelain sink rested in a rough-hewn log countertop, grooved with age and knife marks.

More tree trunk slabs jutted from the kitchen walls to make shelves. Soon they'd hold our spices, canned goods, glasses, dishes, and pots and pans. Against one wall, an antique cupboard with a porcelain ledge that slid out sat empty. I pictured myself using that space to roll out pizza dough and mix ingredients for scones and cookies. A bare bulb hung from the ceiling, scarcely brightening the darkness when Cragg closed the door.

"There's no automatic pilot light," Cragg said as I creaked open the oven door of the cabin's apartment-sized gas cook stove. "You have to light the burners and the oven with a match."

"Where's the fridge?" I asked.

"Oh, it's in that building right outside. We wired that for the refrigerator and hot water tank for the shower. The water in the kitchen is cold, but at least you'll have hot water for showering."

Plastic lawn chairs, folding metal chairs, and a couple of ladder-back wooden chairs clustered around an oak table. Worn planks of cedar created a floor in the dining room and the living room. A window on one wall of the living room let in a bit of light; the spaces around its ledge looked big enough for not only mosquitoes but also the animals that had left their foul smells behind.

"There's a full-sized mattress upstairs in the loft," Cragg said, "and a twin bed, too. Then there's more sleeping space in the little A-frame building outside." He glanced around the cabin as if looking for something. "Oh yeah, there's an outhouse to your left when you go out the front door."

"I think we can make it work," I said. "We're grateful to have a place."

"Yeah, it's tough in the summer with all the part-timers coming back and cabins rented out to tourists. But we'll have this ready for you before you have to leave the Barnharts' so you can get settled in."

We'd known all winter that we'd need to move when school was out in June so that Mike and Nancy and their two boys could return for the summer. Cliff had decided to not rent out his house as he had the previous summer, so we couldn't stay there again. Once the roads and lanes were clear of snow, we had canvassed the valley for signs of vacant cabins and asked everyone for contact information about absentee owners. It seemed all the part-timers were planning to spend all or part of the upcoming summer in Stehekin; no one was interested in our offers to pay rent, move out intermittently for owners' visits, and do repairs or maintenance.

After weeks of dead-ended leads, we'd resigned ourselves to the prospect of renting Robbie's family's house in the woods. Or rather, I had an attitude of resignation about the place Robbie's brothers had built twenty years earlier; Jerry and the kids saw it as just another Stehekin adventure.

The Barnharts had told us we could store many of our belongings in closets for our return in the fall. In the days before we moved into the cabin, I boxed up items we'd use during the summer: the Kitchen-aid mixer, pizza pans, books, games, and our boom box and CDs and tapes. Packing allowed me to procrastinate writing a report for the Health Department about my last consultation visit in the spring. Motivation to finish it came when I realized that once it was completed, I could stash away all my nursing files until the fall.

True to their word, Robbie and Cragg cleaned up the cabin and trapped a pack rat that had nested there. Tammy found a colorful plastic cloth and had put it and a vase of fresh flowers on the dining room table the day we moved in. By the time we filled the kitchen shelves with our staples and our first grocery order of the summer, the place started to look like our own. The dried urine smell of the rat remained, though, regardless of how many scented candles we burned.

One day while making dinner, I remembered first reading our now well-worn copy of the April 1974 issue of *National Geographic*. It featured a story about life in Stehekin in the winter, including a description of the cabin we now called "home." The article pictured Robbie's mom crocheting by kerosene light in the living room. On another page, there was an eleven-year-old Robbie, grinning shyly as she worked bread dough in the same kitchen where I now browned ground beef, chopped onions and tomatoes, and grated cheese for tacos. Friends and visitors often mentioned the article in awe-filled tones.

As my paring knife slipped from my hand and clinked onto the river rock floor, I picked it up with a groan. I was getting more of a taste of what pioneer life was like here, and I wondered how, and why, people did it. Perhaps Robbie's family had left Seattle twenty-five years earlier for the same reasons I'd been drawn to the quiet and solitude of Stehekin. Had they, too, wanted to escape the pace and consumerism of urban life?

Robbie had never volunteered that story and perhaps didn't even know it because she, then, was even younger than Rachel and Matt were when we arrived in Stehekin.

While the meat simmered on the stove, I took the knife and cutting board to the sink. When I turned on the wobbly faucet, air and a few drops of icy water sputtered out. "Dammit," I said, even though there was no one to hear me. This wasn't the first time we'd lost water in the kitchen sink. Our water supply coursed downhill from a creek half-a-mile away through lengths of plastic pipe cobbled together with connectors. Some days the water gushed from the tap; other times, like today, it barely trickled. I turned off the flame under the pan and started my search to trace the pipe's route to the spot where it had worked its way apart or broken. Fortunately that day, the separated joint was only a few feet from the house, and I reconnected the pipe and returned to the kitchen.

"Smells good," Matt said as he and Rachel burst in a few minutes later.

"I'm starved," Rachel said, perspiration underlining the pale red mark her bike helmet left on her forehead.

After Rachel had gotten off work from her dishwashing job at the bakery, she'd met up with Matt at Discovery Bikes, Ron Scutt's summertime bicycle rental business. Matt had succeeded at getting hired there, wiping down bikes after customers returned them.

"Tacos will be ready soon," I said. "Hey, Rachel, how did clean-up at the bakery go?" She'd been on the job just a few days and had already told Robbie she'd like to work more hours.

"There was a ton of sticky pans to wash," she said as she plopped onto a chair at the table. "We got low on cookies, so Tammy showed me how to scoop them. That was fun."

"You'll be baking there before you know it," I said.

"When's Dad getting home?" Matt asked.

"Around eight thirty. We'll eat without him so I can get to bed early. I'm working at the bakery in the morning."

This was the typical routine throughout much of the summer. Both Jerry and I worked full-time, the kids, part-time. Jerry and I tried to coincide our days off, but it was rare that they matched. Many nights I stumbled up the stairs to our sleeping loft just as Jerry came in from returning Ranch dinner guests to the landing.

The dreariness of the cabin and the grind of returning to full-time work added to my growing awareness that my honeymoon with Stehekin was over, or at least was on hiatus. Unlike the valley's tourists who sat drop-jawed at Rainbow Falls and snacked on the bakery's sticky buns while hiking to glacier-capped peaks, all I could focus on was the circumference of our summer home with its listing outhouse, decaying buildings patched together with strips of black plastic, and yard littered with piles of rock, tree stumps, and broken equipment. Going to work before dawn interrupted the morning routine I'd followed in the winter of daily free-writing and study of *The Artist's Way*. I rarely had time for meditation or introspection, and when I did, my thoughts swirled with questions about what I was meant to do with my life. Our Sunday morning gatherings for silent worship had disbanded for the summer, too.

One evening after work, Jerry found me curled up in the only upholstered chair in the house. The words I might have scrawled into my journal spilled out of my mouth.

"I think I've discovered my limit for roughing it," I said.

"Yeah?" he asked, kissing the top of my head.

"I guess I'm not as committed to a simple lifestyle as I'd like to think. I can deal with the outhouse and the fridge in the out-building and heating water on the stove to wash dishes..."

"But..."

"But the dark, tripping on that rock floor in the kitchen, and the pack rat smell are getting to me." I picked up Skoshi and stroked her satiny gray fur and crooked tail. "The last straw was when I realized the cats can get in and out of the house through a hole in the wall." The plaster that Robbie's brothers had chinked between the log rounds of varying diameters that formed the cabin's wall now crumbled into little mounds inside and out. No need for a cat door.

"I know it's not the greatest, but at least it's only temporary," Jerry said.

"You're gone most of the time, and I'm tired of dealing with broken water pipes and trying to sleep when everybody else is downstairs in the living room."

Tears surfaced, and Jerry pulled me up off the chair and gave me a hug.

"Everybody else is on vacation and we're working harder than ever. I feel like we have to cater to everyone and that we're 'on' all the time, answering questions, entertaining, guiding..." I buried my chin in Jerry's shoulder as tears bunched in my throat. I felt his strong arms tighten around the small of my back. "If this is what we have to do to live a simpler life, I don't know if I can do it." My study of the Quaker value of simplicity hadn't quite prepared me for Robbie's cabin.

Over my snuffles he murmured, "You head up to bed. I'll finish clean-up so you can get to sleep."

"Thanks, honey," I said. I brushed his lips with mine, not able to muster the energy for anything more passionate, and trudged out the cabin door for the outhouse.

*   *   *

It took a while for me to get back into the rhythm of the bakery, but soon I regained the feeling of competence I'd developed by the end of the season the previous October. Although I still had to refer to my butter-stained notes occasionally, I started this season already knowing how much batter to scoop into the muffin tins and that Robbie's scone recipe called for milk and the orange twist dough required cream. This season I not only knew that the proof box was the warm metal cabinet where we put the yeasted breads and pastries to rise, but also how much the dough should have risen before transferring the pans from there into the oven.

The first summer, the bakery had been unfamiliar territory for me, and I'd felt as insecure as a beginning baker as I had as a new supervisor at the health department a couple of years earlier. Although I knew I'd never reach the skill level of Robbie and Tammy, I believed I'd earned my spot behind the bench next to them as a member of the team. Until Donnalynn arrived.

I remembered Donnalynn's friendly smile from the previous summer when she worked at the Lodge store. Although she was a good fifteen years older than I was, she had a lot of energy packed into her petite frame. When I heard she'd been hired by Robbie to be a part-time baker, I assumed she'd be a good addition to our all-female crew.

Robbie worked the jigsaw puzzle of the staffing schedule so that she or Tammy would be there every day to decide which pastries we'd make and how many loaves of bread and batches of scones, twists, and cookies we'd produce. One of them also had to be on duty to fill the pie order that the Ranch called in by radio every morning around eleven. I worked my way up to mix fruit for berry pies and the syrup, brown sugar, butter, and walnuts for Washington Nut Pie, but Robbie never entrusted me, or anyone but Tammy, with the flaky crusts. When Jerry or any of the other Ranch shuttle drivers came to pick up the pies to take them up-valley in time for dinner, we'd stack them gently in recycled plastic milk crates outfitted with custom-made plywood stands. Customers stepped aside and bowed their heads reverently as the drivers hefted their cargo out the bakery doors.

On busy weekends and holidays, both Tammy and Robbie worked, along with Donnalynn or me, to keep up with the production levels needed to feed the bigger crowds. When one of them had a day off, though, Donnalynn and I were assigned to the same shift to assist whichever of the veteran bakers was on the schedule. As a returning baker, I watched Robbie and Tammy train Donnalynn as they had done for me a year earlier. What she lacked in skill, she made up for in self-confidence and speed. It shouldn't have been a surprise that my attention to detail and her desire to set time records would clash.

One morning, as we scurried to transfer muffins and Danish from baking pans to serving platters for the display case, I slid a baking sheet filled with orange twists that Donnalynn had made from the cooling rack onto the stainless steel prep table. This was the last day of a seven-day stretch without a break for me, and I was feeling the fatigue of too many early mornings. The edge of my spatula bounced off the blackened, crisp marmalade filling that had oozed from one of the pastries onto the baking sheet. No amount of coaxing could ease the gooey grip, and the buttery treat broke in half.

"Donnalynn, I think you put too much marmalade in the twists today. I can't get them off the sheet."

"Oh, that's what makes them good. People love them when they've got lots of filling."

"Maybe so," I said, gritting my teeth as I wiggled the spatula and pried the parchment paper away from the sticky glob around another one. "But it sure makes it a pain to get them off the pan in one piece and into the case. Could you please go a little lighter in the future?"

Donnalynn shrugged, sighed, and twisted her mouth into a grimacing smile. I fumed as she rolled her eyes and said, "I'll try."

I spent the rest of the morning sweating over what I viewed as her sloppiness and disregard for the effect of her actions on her co-workers. I kept hoping Robbie would intervene with corrections and reminders to Donnalynn about the baking techniques I knew she'd taught to both of us. As Robbie remained silent, all I could think was, *Thank God I'm off tomorrow. I need a break from working with Donnalynn.*

Around noon, Robbie slid the last of the pies in the oven.

"OK," she said, "you guys can start cleanup."

I untied my apron and pitched it into the bin Robbie kept on the back porch for dirty laundry. I grabbed one of the pastry knives from the bench, slumped down to the floor on all fours, and started to loosen up bits of flour and butter. An ache crept into my lower back and marched up to my neck and head. I noticed Donnalynn had started her crawl in front of the refrigerators and was scraping her way toward the end of the bench at a sprinter's pace.

I tried to remember how many cups of coffee Donnalyn had swigged that morning as we baked; either she was speeded up on caffeine or was being as casual with the cleanup as I felt she'd been with the marmalade. When our paths intersected in the middle of the bakery, Donnalyn drew her five-foot-two-inch frame to its full height as she slapped her bench knife down on the butcher-block table.

"I'm tired of you harping at me about how to do my baking," she said. Although I was a good five inches taller, from my vantage point on my hands and knees, Donnalynn towered over me; I felt like Cinderella to her wicked step-sister.

"Sorry," I said, "I don't mean to harp." I rested back on my heels but still had to crane my neck to make eye contact with her. "I do wish, though, you'd take it a little easy with the marmalade and the glazes. It really makes it hard for whoever has to take things off the baking sheets."

"I don't know who you think you are, telling me what to do. If Robbie doesn't like it, she'll tell me."

My mouth dropped open as I looked up at Donnalynn's eyes, bloodshot now with anger. I hadn't recognized that all morning, resentment must have been brewing in her slight, graying body. *This is crazy*, I thought to myself. *Get up off your knees!* I stood up, looked around to see if any customers were at the counter, and felt my face start to flush. "I'm not sure what's going on here, Donnalynn. I think we need to talk it over."

"Nah, talking doesn't do any good. Just get off my back."

"Girls, girls," Robbie said. More heat flooded my cheeks as I brushed past Donnalynn to get a broom to sweep up my debris. Neither of us said a word to each other for the rest of our shift.

As Donnalynn brisked through the screen door after cleanup, I followed close behind.

"Donnalynn, I really don't want to leave things like this," I said.

She whirled around, the same scowl on her face as I'd seen while I was kneeling on the floor. "Just drop it," she said. "Everybody thinks you've got to talk things out. That's bullshit. You just do your job, and I'll do mine. We don't need to talk about anything."

"But..." She was out of earshot before I could get out any more words.

That night, I vented my frustration to Jerry.

"It's been a long time since anyone has talked to me like that," I said. "I'd sure like to clear the air with her, but I don't think there's much chance of that."

"Sounds like she made it pretty clear she doesn't want to talk."

"I'm also embarrassed Robbie saw that interaction," I said. "I feel like I'm in a turf battle with Donnalynn, and it's so silly. They're just baked goods!"

"Well, you're tired, and you've worked really hard to learn how to do things the way Robbie likes. I'm sure she knows what a good employee you are."

"I hope so. I never expected to have this kind of friction at the bakery. I still have so much to learn about dealing with conflict. I don't like it any better here than I did at the health department. At least I finally got up off of my knees and talked to her at eye level."

"Don't be hard on yourself. Sounds like you handled a tough situation well. And now you have a couple of days off."

"Yeah, and fortunately, I don't have to work with Donnalynn for awhile again, either."

That night, I didn't bother to set the alarm, and I kept reading until my eyes closed and my book fell to the floor. Not even the buzz of the mosquitoes penetrated my fatigue.

CHAPTER 16

Tired of Not Knowing

A CLINKING SOUND DREW MY ATTENTION to where I parked my bicycle then brought me to a frozen halt. A juvenile black bear perched on a mound of dirt left over from digging for the water line to the house. He (or she, I didn't try to determine which) seemed oblivious to my presence as he batted a discarded root beer can with his front paws. I tiptoed back into the cabin and took up an observation post at the kitchen window. Jerry, Rachel, and Matt were all at work, so I studied the bear, knowing they'd expect a detailed report.

I realized I was holding my breath as I watched the bear turn the can end-over-end-over-end and roll it in the ground. I wasn't frightened, really, remembering that although black bears are omnivores, they prefer huckleberries, wasps' nests, and the grubs I'd seen one pawing for in a muddy spot by our leaking water pipe. Still, I was grateful for the wall between us. His paws added another crease to the can as he put it to his mouth. I tapped on the window glass, hoping to motivate the bear back into the woods; I had to get on my bike soon if I was going to make it to the post office before the boat arrived. Sunlight gleamed on the black and root-beer-brown of the bear's coat and glinted off his root-beer-dampened snout. He didn't even look my way.

I grabbed a pot and spoon from the dish drainer, pushed open the cabin door, and marched outside, banging the spoon against the bottom of the pot. The bear looked up for a moment, then returned to the can. I clanged some more, sang a song to the rhythm, then shouted, "Shoo!" The bear lifted his head slowly, let the root beer can roll off the dirt mound, and ambled away from the cabin and toward the trees. I made a U-turn to the cabin, stashed the pot and spoon, and scooped up my stack of outgoing mail.

With our decision to stay in Stehekin for another year, we knew we had to make the most of the earning time in the summer, what the locals called the "100-day season." I was grateful we were spared forest fires that second summer and that tourist traffic picked up, but that meant I had several stretches of seven straight days of work. Jerry's workload was heavy as well. In addition to driving the shuttle bus for the Ranch, he added some hours working for the Park Service in the maintenance department, a move that increased his chances of intermittent work in the off-season.

Even the kids got a taste of the realities of making a living in a remote, tourist community. On days that Matt wasn't working at Mr. Scutt's bicycle rental stand, he earned a little money juggling on the bakery lawn.

"Woohoo," he called out one night as I tried to get to sleep. I'd heard the clink of coins as he dumped them from the hat he used for his bakery busking. "I made thirty-two bucks today!"

Rachel did a different kind of juggling with dishwashing at the bakery, housekeeping at a bed and breakfast, and occasional babysitting.

Now, as my yellow bike wobbled down the lane and onto the paved road, I replayed the scene of the bear in our yard. *This will make a good story the next time I go to Bellingham,* I mused. A steady stream of pickups and cars slowed to go around me as I joined the procession to get to the post office before Don loaded the day's mail into canvas sacks for the boat.

Bellingham. I hadn't thought much about it since the day weeks earlier I'd also hustled to the post office to mail the report from my last consultation at the health department. I remembered the relief I'd felt as I stashed a box of nursing files alongside snow boots and winter gear in a closet at the Barnhart house. And I remembered the creases in Carole's forehead that day in the spring when I'd talked with her in my former office, reports and phone messages covering every inch of my old desk.

The story of my bear encounter entertained the locals as we waited for Don to sort the day's incoming mail and fill our mailboxes. I knew that all of them had their own stories of black bears raiding the freezers on their porches, stripping their apple trees clean, and upending garbage cans with the same ease that "my" bear had flipped the soda can, but they listened respectfully. I even got a grunt out of Wally, a sure sign he'd tuned in to my tale.

As tourists and seasonal crews circulated through the bakery on hot summer days, Donnalynn and I succeeded at avoiding any more conflicts. Robbie came to rely on me to do all the baking duties except the pies. References to my "crooked as hell" pizza cutting were all spoken in the past tense as I mastered that task, too. I continued to bask in customers' hyperbolic praise of the cinnamon rolls and Danish pastries that caused their eyes to glaze over as they stood in front of the display case. Although I never tired of their exclamations over the butter and sugar smells that greeted them, by August my enthusiasm flagged.

I welcomed the start of the school year, the cooler daytime temperatures, and our return to the comforts of the Barnhart house. Shortly after Labor Day, we moved back in, Rachel and Matt settled in to their upstairs bedrooms, and Jerry and I unpacked the boxes we'd stored for the summer.

"I can't believe all this stuff we have," I said to Jerry as he stacked books and games back on the living room shelves and I returned our espresso machine and Kitchen Aid mixer to the kitchen counter. "Why can't we—how can we—cut down some of this?"

"Yeah, seems like we still have a lot to learn about simplifying," Jerry said.

I spoke out loud my questions about trimming our belongings; I raised others in my morning pages as I returned to that daily practice once the kids were back in school. My fatigue from the summer baking schedule convinced me that the life of a baker wasn't for me. I'd had sales of my block print cards and calendars at the Craft Cabin, but I still didn't feel I could claim the title of artist. I turned to Natalie Goldberg's *Writing Down the Bones* and adopted her practice of daily timed writing exercises, only to question if this would get me any closer to published writing and to wonder if my drive for publication was motivated by my unease with calling myself a writer. And, uncertainty remained still about how, or if, I was to continue work as a nurse.

Rachel and Matt's return to school offered some diversion. Along with their classmate John, they were now among the three respected eighth-graders, and they came home the first day full of news and plans.

"We had flowers on our desks today because we're the oldest students," Rachel reported.

"And we got the desks in the corner this year," Matt said. "Mine is right by Mr. Scutt's desk."

I looked at Jerry and raised my eyebrows. I wondered if this desk location indicated Ron was concerned about Matt's behavior and whether we'd be getting another letter in the coming weeks.

That night, after the kids went up to bed and while Jerry finished kitchen cleanup, I slid under the sheets of our double bed. As I flipped the pages of a book I'd just gotten from the library, I laughed out loud.

"What's so funny?" Jerry asked a few minutes later as he closed the bedroom door and snuggled in next to me.

"No mosquitoes buzzing my ears," I said, laughing again.

"Mmm, that is nice, isn't it?" Jerry said, his warm breath on my earlobe a welcome alternative.

"Nice to hear that the kids had such a good first day at school, too," I said.

"Yeah, they seem pretty happy about being eighth-graders." Jerry scooted closer and draped an arm over my chest.

"I don't remember them ever sounding so excited about school assignments at Whatcom," I said, turning toward his embrace.

"Nope, and not nearly as excited as I am about being able to close our door and have some privacy again," he said.

*   *   *

WHILE I COUNTED DOWN THE DAYS to the closing of the bakery in October, I looked forward to what we'd learned the previous year were the fall traditions in Stehekin. I again helped with the School Day at the Bakery overseeing the making of pizza and cinnamon rolls. The annual Pizza Feed the next day marked the end of the Stehekin Pastry Company season, and that year's downpour didn't dampen the crowd's spirits or inhibit live fiddle music on the porch.

While the rainstorm hadn't cancelled the bakery festivities, it did threaten the annual school outing to Horseshoe Basin. Finally the sun broke through, and Ron gave the thumbs up for the day trip. The next morning, I huddled with the ten students and a couple of other chaperones in the bed of Ron's old blue Dodge pickup for the twenty-mile drive to the trailhead at Cottonwood. I pulled my stocking cap down toward my neck and smiled at Rachel, the wind whipping her blond hair across her grin.

A couple of hours later, Ron's pickup lurched to a stop at Cottonwood and the kids scrambled toward the trail, with Justin, the school's youngest student, at the head of the line. I followed at the end of the string of kids and listened to their chatter as they started the two-mile trek toward the ultimate destination, the abandoned Black Warrior Mine. As the sun warmed the air, the kids' calls for water stops got closer together. During one of those pauses, my gaze turned to the large cirque between Sahale, Boston, Ripsaw Ridge, and Buckner mountains. Waterfalls there, cascading from the glaciers above, made lacy patterns against the dark gray stone. A *ceanothus*-scented breeze swept across the horseshoe-shaped basin, cooling us after our switch-backing journey.

Rachel had told me she'd been looking forward to again exploring the mine, and she was the first to pull on a sweatshirt, grab a flashlight, and step into the icy dampness of the mine's entrance. As in the previous year, though, I couldn't muster the courage to venture past the room just inside the mineshaft that historians believe miners used for warming and cooking. I waited there, my eyes adjusting to the darkness, and listened to the echoing voices of Rachel, Matt, and the rest of the kids. Back in Ron's truck on the way home, they chattered about balancing on old cart rails to avoid muddy puddles on the mine floor and how the eighth-graders needed to stoop down in places where the shaft barely cleared their heads. Rachel sat up a little taller as she reported climbing up into the concave pit at the end of the mine and touching the back of the wall.

*   *   *

IN ADDITION TO OUR FALL ROUTINE, I made several trips downlake for nursing activities. First was a presentation at a workshop for public health nurses consulting with child-care programs, then a few days giving flu shots in Bellingham, and finally flying to San Diego for the annual meeting of the American Public Health Association. In all those places, I easily slipped back in to my nursing role and savored a sense of serving and having valued expertise.

One evening after I returned from San Diego, as Jerry and I started to clear dinner dishes, he asked how it had been for me to be so immersed again in nursing.

"It was good," I said, "although I missed not having as much time to write or work on block prints."

"How was it seeing your public health buddies?" Jerry asked.

"It's funny," I said. " I expected people might be critical of my pulling back, but everyone was interested in what I'm doing here and what it's like to live in Stehekin."

"That's good, right?"

I squirted dish soap into the soup bowls Jerry had stacked in the sink and turned the faucet to hot. After our summer in the mosquito cabin, I still relished water steaming from the tap instead of heating it on the stove. "Yeah, but now that I'm back, I feel like nobody here has any awareness of me as a nurse and couldn't relate to what I've just been doing downlake. I just want to know who I'm supposed to be."

"Isn't that part of what you're figuring out while we're here?" Jerry said as he paused from dish drying and leaned against the counter.

Many times I'd chastised him for not being able to talk and dry dishes at the same time, but that night I didn't care. I was working to hold back tears. "I just thought I'd have some clarity about work by now," I said. "When I'm with other nurses like I was at the workshops, I feel excited about all the good that I think we do in public health. But then I remember how frustrated I felt at the health department, and I wonder just what it is I'm called to do." Suds slopped onto the counter as I scrubbed the soup pot. "I'm so tired of not knowing."

"Honey, you've got time, you don't have to have it all figured out just yet."

He was right, I knew, but as I looked out the kitchen window into the darkness of the night, the figuring out seemed as far out of my reach as that back wall in the Black Warrior Mine.

CHAPTER 17

Leaning Into It

T HAT YEAR, SNOW CAME TO THE VALLEY FLOOR in early November, followed by warmer temperatures and then days and days of heavy rain. Rocks and boulders in the summer-dried riverbed disappeared as the river swelled. What had been a tranquil trickle of flowing water just days before was now a roar we could hear whenever we opened the door. As we prepared for another Thanksgiving, we kept close watch on the river inching up its banks. This year, the Amber-Oliver family would make it to Stehekin, along with the Evergreens, for our traditional celebration.

One day on my way to pick up groceries at the landing, I saw Wally working on his truck. I stopped to talk about the rising river and my fears that our friends might not be able to make it for the holiday.

"Yeah, this reminds me of Thanksgiving of '90," Wally reminisced. "When I came back from downlake, my cabin was surrounded by water. It got clear up to the doorway before it went down."

Great, I thought. I didn't know whether to worry that our friends wouldn't be able to make it or, that they would, and then the two adult couples and the four kids might get stranded in Stehekin. Fortunately, the rain let up, the *Lady of the Lake* didn't break down, there were no mix-ups with our grocery order, and our friends arrived safely. Once again we feasted, reminisced about earlier days, complained about the state of the world, played board games, and ate some more. The kids weren't deterred by the rain's effect on the snow and spent hours playing outside. Their jackets, snow pants, boots, and gloves barely had time to dry by the woodstove before they were ready to go out again.

While we adults had talked after Thanksgiving dinner, Nick had come in from playing outside and motioned to DeeDee to follow him upstairs.

"Iris, could you come up?" she called, a few minutes later.

I heard her voice from Matt's room as I got to the top of the stairs. "We're in here."

Nick was stretched out on Matt's bed. DeeDee was kneeling next to him stroking his right arm; his left arm was draped over his eyes. I knelt beside DeeDee.

"Nick's been kind of stressed out at school," DeeDee said, "and his doctor started him on an antidepressant. He says his stomach hurts, and I'm wondering if it's the medicine."

While I scrolled through my memory about medication side effects, my mind also was trying to process this new information about Nick's depression. I looked at the slice of his pale face that wasn't covered and asked him some questions about how he was feeling. Inwardly, I wondered how this could be happening to a kid who seemed so much like my own children; to a family so much like us. If Nick could be depressed, could my kids? If our friends were struggling with their child's mental health, could that happen to us?

After DeeDee and I spent some time with Nick and listened to his worries about his stomachache, he returned to playing with the kids. Throughout the rest of their stay, I watched him as unobtrusively as I could, looking for signs of a reaction to his anti-depressant or of whatever troubles he carried inside. Everything seemed as it always had been, and my only advice to DeeDee was to continue to monitor Nick's behavior and let his doctor know if the stomach upset persisted.

The rain returned on Sunday morning just as the two families packed their belongings and we loaded up the Suburban to take them to the boat landing.

"It was so good to have you all here," I said as we shared farewell hugs. "I think you might be getting out just in time, though. Looks like we're in for more rain."

And we were, with nonstop torrents pounding our metal roof and saturating the yard; any spot bare of snow turned into a puddle. Now, the river flow that usually soothed me, echoed thunderous, tumbling boulders and crashing, hundred-foot tall cedars and pines, their roots torn from the banks by the pressure of the current. Late one afternoon midweek, the river exploded over the bank at the end of Company Creek Road, and gushed through the foundation of the Avery cabin just beyond our house. As we watched the brown froth surge down the road, we saw our part-time neighbor, artist Sandy Walker, wading through it toward our house.

"Water's starting to come into my studio," Sandy said. "Can you help me make a barricade?"

All four of us bundled up in raincoats and snow boots and scavenged for anything that might block the flow. An hour later, our makeshift dam of logs, rocks, and discarded sheet metal was diverting the river's overflow away from the studio and down the road.

Before slogging back to our house, we inched as close to the roiling river as we dared. As full-sized cedars rumbled past, I wondered how one of my favorite trees was faring. Early in our relocation to Stehekin, I spotted it just beyond Harlequin Bridge and called it my "lean into it" tree. The cedar stretched its lower third over the riverbank before curving the rest of its height gracefully up toward the sky. Five roots, as thick as a grown man's thighs, sprawled from the tree's stringy-barked trunk and clawed into the soil. Half-a-dozen branches reached out across the river as if in a tug-of-war with the roots to keep the cedar upright and anchored. Could it survive the thrashing water now gnawing at the banks of the Stehekin?

"Hey guys," Rachel said as we sat down to dinner, "it's stopped raining."

"Yay," cheered Matt.

"I wouldn't get too excited yet," Jerry said. "The river's so full we'll need lots of days without rain to make a difference."

That wouldn't happen for a while, as the rain returned during the night.

The next morning, Jerry, the kids and I ventured down Company Creek Road to see the effects of the night's deluge. After about half a mile, just before Jim and Rene Courtney's place, we could go no further. Water had burst over the embankment.

I shuffled back a few feet from the raw river edge, keeping my eyes on the new arm of the Stehekin surging down the middle of the road. The same road that wound from our house for four miles beside the Stehekin, then across Harlequin Bridge to connect us to the five miles of paved road leading to the ferry landing, the head of Lake Chelan, and the rest of the world. Now, this link had been split by a torrent of mud-brown, churning water, so deep I couldn't see the rock roadbed that surely lay underneath. Cut off from friends, neighbors, the school, mail, and groceries, I huddled with Jerry and the kids, all of us staring at the galloping currents.

"What we need is for the temperature to drop and turn this rain into snow," Jerry said as we sloshed back to the house. Probably nobody wanted that more than Dan Wilsey, whose plight we listened to later that morning over the Park Service two-way radio. A familiar voice interrupted the radio's crackle.

"We need to get the Wilseys out."

Burton Karapostoles, one of the maintenance crew, was reporting in after surveying the damage in front of the Wilsey house and the shop where Dan repaired nearly all the vehicles in Stehekin. Dan's place was about the same distance upriver as ours, but on the opposite side; we clustered around the radio to hear this report.

For once I was glad to have the radio in our house. Earlier in the fall when Jerry had been hired as a part-time maintenance employee, he'd received the radio to stay in touch with the rest of the crew working in the valley. As much as I treasured the absence of phones, television, and newspapers in Stehekin, that week, the radio sat prominently on the kitchen counter, humming with news of the rising river.

"I'm on the front end loader," Burton said to his supervisor, Ray Lawless, "and we moved that big cottonwood that fell across the road by the Danielson place. I can't tell how much of the road washed away after we moved it."

I tried to picture the scene as Burton went on. "The loader lurched when we got to the spot where the cottonwood came down. Looks like there's not much road left on the river side."

Dan took a turn on the radio. "I moved all the vehicles to higher ground. Our place is an island now. I don't think I want to wait around here with Karen and the boys watching the water come up!" The radio snapped and fuzzed as Dan awaited a reply.

"This is as suspenseful as any made-for-television movie," I said, trying for a little levity to break the tension. The kids, their eyes wide, hovered around the table. Ray's voice came on, giving the go-ahead for Burton to evacuate Dan's family, and we listened until we heard they made it out safely. It would be a few days later that we learned that Karen and Dan had hung on to each side of the rig while two of their boys cuddled beside Burton in the cab, and the other three crouched in the machine's bucket.

Once the radio conversation between Ray and Burton ended, we again heard Ray's voice, this time calling for Jerry.

"How are things up by your place?" Ray asked.

"Well, right before Jim and Rene's house, there's about a fifty-yard gap in Company Creek Road," Jerry said.

"Maybe we can get over there in a bit with the front end loader," Ray said.

Jerry shook his head and pressed the radio's talk button. "Ray, the road is gone."

"Yeah, I heard you, but don't you think we could get through with the front end loader?"

"The road is *completely* gone," Jerry repeated, this time his voice a few decibels louder. His knuckles whitened as his right hand clutched the radio. "There's no way anything can get through until the river goes down."

The power of this force humbled me. How many times had that river flooded, reminding the residents of its valley we had intruded on its home? We might think we know best where roads should go or houses should be built, but the river follows its own wisdom, has its own idea about its course, and thus ours. I had come to Stehekin to wrestle with both my need for control as well as the ways I'd disengaged from the world to protect myself from urban overload and work stress. The flood's fury reconnected me to the earth. The water frothing between the banks carried the rains, the melted snows, the ancient glacial melt that forced the Stehekin to escape its borders and eat away at the bend in the road. Now a big chunk of road joined this flow of history, mingled with old and new waters, mixed with boulders and pines that rushed down the swollen river, to the head of the lake, bound to get to Chelan, the Columbia, and the sea before I would. While the Stehekin raged a record 19,000 cubic square feet of water every minute, there was nothing for us to do but wait, stranded at our end of Company Creek Road.

Along with the boulders and trees, the river washed away power poles and lines, leaving us without electricity during the flood's climax. Fortunately, we'd heeded our neighbors' advice to fill our bathtub with water in anticipation of the loss of our electric pump for the well. We had plenty of firewood for the barrel stove that warmed the house. A full tank of propane fueled our cooking stove to heat the food we kept cold in an ice chest on the front porch. Our days were filled with basic survival chores as well as monitoring the river's course, so it didn't matter that the sun disappeared around four in the afternoon. After dinner preparation, cleanup, and a little reading by the light of candles and kerosene lamps, we were all ready for sleep.

Three days after the road disappeared, the water receded enough for Cragg to drive his bulldozer into the woods beyond the washout to punch out a temporary road. Now crews could get in to replace the missing power poles and string new lines to restore electricity. Life began to return to normal.

When we got permission to drive across the temporary road, my family and I enthusiastically piled into the Suburban. I was eager to reunite with friends from throughout the valley, knowing there would be stories to hear, and our own to tell. Jerry drove slower than usual down the narrow, winding road, not knowing what hazards from the river's rampage might stop us. Its surge had created gullies, cleaned out fall debris, and scattered firewood, toys, barrels, shovels, rakes, and ladders far from their homes.

We'd heard that the approaches to Harlequin Bridge had taken a beating. I held my breath as we neared the bend just before it. The sky was blue, but the coffee-and- cream-colored river bubbling past like soup at a hard boil still taunted both sides of the road and the bridge's underside. Paths we'd walked to the river's edge had been nibbled away. Cedars and pines from further upriver littered the beach at Harlequin Campground. My eyes focused to the left, just beyond the bridge's span, to the bank across from us. Still "leaning into it," my cedar clung to the river's edge, reaching toward the sun while remaining firmly rooted in the rock and soil. I let out my breath and leaned a bit more into life's requirement to both hold on and let go.

CHAPTER 18

Bad News Always Finds You

ONCE ELECTRICITY WAS RESTORED AFTER THE FLOOD, I noticed just how much I appreciated the light on my nightstand for bedtime reading, not having to haul water from the river to flush the toilet, and the pleasure of playing the tape deck again. One afternoon as I carved linoleum blocks for prints for Christmas cards, I listened to a recording of "Morning Edition" sent to us by friends. A few minutes into the show, Bob Edwards' voice was interrupted by the sound of squabbling upstairs. I couldn't make out the words, but I could hear Matt mumbling and Rachel's voice turning to a rant. A few minutes later, she swung the door from upstairs open, her force making it rumble like the Stehekin had a few days earlier.

"Ughhh," Rachel spouted as she crossed her arms over her chest.

I set down my carving knife and looked at her. "What's up?"

"I can't stand living with him," she said, flinging her body into the chair across from me. "He always acts like he knows everything, like he's so much smarter than everybody else."

Her bangs swayed to reveal deep creases in her forehead, and she blinked away tears. I knelt beside her and put my arms around her shoulders as they started to quiver.

"Oh honey, you and Matt are so different. You like to talk everything out, and he mulls stuff over in his head."

"Yeah, and then when he does say something, it's like whatever I think doesn't matter."

"How about if you both cool off for a bit? Look at these blocks I'm carving and tell me what you think."

I set Rachel to work making sample prints of the snowy cedar image I'd carved on a block. As she spread black ink onto a piece of glass and then glided a roller over it and onto the block, I headed upstairs.

"Matt," I said, tapping my knuckles on his bedroom door.

"Yeah," he said, as I pushed the door open. He sat on his bed, his math book propped on his knees.

"Sounds like you and Rachel had a tough conversation earlier."

"I was just trying to help her with her math," he said. "Then she got all huffy when I told her she wasn't doing it right."

I perched on the edge of his bed and put my hand on his knee. "Well, sometimes it's not so much what you say as how you say it. You can be pretty blunt."

"But she just goes on and on and acts like she's my mom." He stuck his pencil in the crease of the book and snapped it shut. The book thudded as he tossed it to the foot of the bed.

"You two do have different ways of communicating, that's for sure."

Matt folded his arms across his chest and focused on the wall behind me. "I'm tired of just being with Rachel. I can't wait until the rain stops and I can hang out with Mugs again."

"Yeah, I think we're all suffering from cabin fever. I bet Murphy would enjoy a game of catch if you're ready to take a break from math."

By the time I returned to the kitchen, Rachel had filled the table with cards. "I think we should take some of these with us to Seattle for Christmas," she said as she peeled another print off the block. She didn't even look up as Matt and Murphy sprinted past and out the back door.

*   *   *

Jerry's family had enjoyed the previous Christmas in Stehekin, but we all knew emotions would be fragile for this first holiday season without Windsor. Jerry's cousin and her husband offered to host everyone at their home in Seattle, so once life returned to normal after the flood, we filled the evenings and weekends again making and wrapping gifts to send to my mom and Steve and to take to Seattle. This year, we were more efficient in our search for a Christmas tree, having set some limits on size and how long we'd spend on our hunt.

As on so many trips downlake before, the further we got from the Stehekin Landing, the glacier-smoothed lakeshore, and views of the "three Bs" (Buckner, Booker, and Boston peaks), the more my breaths shortened. Moments after our descent from Stevens Pass, there was more green and wet than snow, more cars streaming west than east. The closer we got to the city, my right foot twitched as if ready to apply the brakes. By the time we exited Highway 2 and wound our way through the drizzle along the north end of Seattle's Lake Washington, I was feeling very far from home.

"Hey, look at that building," Rachel called from the backseat as we waited for the light at a busy intersection near Jerry's cousin's house. I snorted as I read the metal script over the main entrance—*Uplake Building*.

This year, there wouldn't be any cross-country skiing, no snowball fights, and no power outages. There *would* be orange twists, card games, and multiple trips to the grocery store for forgotten ingredients. And there would be laughter and tears as we reminisced about Windsor wearing his "Gadget King" sweatshirt the previous Christmas morning and his valiant climb to the top of Boris' Bluff.

"We may be near the *Uplake Building*," I said to Jerry one morning as we walked a rain-dampened, paved path between the city street and Lake Washington, "but this is definitely *downlake*." I raised my voice over the sound of cars on the street and a float plane jockeying into position to take off from the lake. "I wonder where we'll celebrate next year."

"Maybe we can have everyone come to Lopez," Jerry said.

"That would be nice, as long as we can find a place to live there. When we get back to Stehekin, I need to talk to Robbie. Her brother's fiancée told me that her sister has a rental house on Lopez."

"Really? What are the chances of that? Maybe we can check it out on spring break…make sure there aren't any pack rats."

"At least there won't be mosquitoes," I said, sidestepping a puddle pooled on the pavement. "And none of this traffic."

"Right," Jerry said, "more like Stehekin but with phones, a grocery store, and a high school."

I watched the floatplane disappear into the gray clouds. "We've still got some good months and another summer ahead of us in Stehekin," I said. "I'm not ready to start thinking about leaving just yet."

The upcoming summer seemed very far off when we returned to Stehekin and a snowy January. As during the previous winter, the kids' involvement in school, Jerry's attention to maintaining household systems, and the near-silence of the muffling snow opened hours for my inward reflection. Writings and exercises of Julia Cameron and Matthew Fox continued to support me in my seeking the work I was called to. From the stack of books I'd crated for winter reading, I pulled Thomas Moore's *Care of the Soul*, finding wisdom and guidance to weave my desires for both solitude and service.

I remained unclear what form that balance would take once we left Stehekin, so I continued to journal my questions and work them in my mind during walks and skiing the groomed, cross-country trails at Buckner Orchard. Sunshine often glinted on the snowy bedspread tucked around the apple trees as I poked my ski poles through the white crust and glided along the tracks. The questioning voice in my head and an occasional poof of snow dropping off a branch were the only sounds.

One afternoon in mid-March, a Park Service ranger pulled into the drive and handed me two slips of paper. They looked just like the "While You Were Away" phone message notes the secretary would clip by my name at the sign-in board at the health department. The Park Service office had a phone, and obviously someone had called there to contact us.

I had welcomed the absence of telephones in Stehekin. Without them, there would be no one calling to offer us carpet cleaning and no dinnertime interruptions by requests for donations or political campaigns urging my vote. There'd also be no teary calls from my mom challenging our judgment to live so remotely or sharing worries about her digestion or Steve's diabetes. Still, I knew it was a strain for her to not be able to pick up the phone whenever she needed reassurance that we were all okay.

"What if something happens and I can't get a hold of you?" she'd asked that first time Jerry and I had vacationed in Stehekin. She questioned us each time over the ten years that we returned, and again when we told her we were moving there. The satellite phone at the landing that we could call out on wasn't much consolation; she wanted to be able to phone us in an emergency.

I admit, that was one worry I also had carried to Stehekin when we made the plan to move there. But since receiving hand-delivered evacuation notices our first summer and, the following spring that message on our windshield to call Jerry's mom, I'd discovered that bad news always finds you. In an odd way, I was reassured.

That day, as I clutched the folded notes in my hand, my first thought was that these were messages to call Jerry at his mom's house in Junction City. Now, a year after Windsor's death, Florence had decided to sell the house the two of them had lived in the forty-five years they'd been married. Jerry had been there for the past week, helping Florence empty out Windsor's shop. For days, she and Jerry filled barrels and bins with tools and tractor and car parts Windsor had accumulated over seventy-eight years. As he rationalized, "you never know when you might need something." Now, Florence knew she wouldn't need this stuff, and Jerry helped her organize it to sell.

But neither of these messages was from Jerry or his mom. One was from Ann, a Seattle friend, and the other was from DeeDee. Both said to call. I couldn't imagine why they'd be trying to get in touch with us. What could be so important that they'd tracked down the Park Service number?

After the kids got home from school, we ate an early dinner, and Rachel and I drove the seven miles from our house to the phone at the ferry landing. Matt opted to stay at home by the warm fire.

The closer we got to the little yellow A-frame that housed the telephone, the more nervous I became about why these friends were trying to reach us. I wondered if they had heard something from Jerry, if there was some problem, and he needed their help to contact us. That didn't seem logical, but the real reason for the calls made even less sense.

I don't remember why I decided to try DeeDee first, but it was her number I tapped on the phone as Rachel and I stood shivering in the cool March air. When DeeDee answered, she sounded different. I assumed it was a poor connection with the satellite feed, but as soon as I told DeeDee it was me calling, I could hear her sob.

"Nick committed suicide," she said. Even with the delays caused by the slow feed and DeeDee's tears, the words were coming too fast. "Last night . . . he took an overdose . . . of his antidepressants."

I reached for Rachel and drew her close to my trembling body. "No, DeeDee," I said. "No."

My dinner churned in my belly; I feared I would throw up. I leaned against the cold wall and lowered myself to the cement floor. My gaze rested at the bottom edge of the phone booth's window with its view onto the lake; the pine-dotted rock face jutting up from the opposite shore was barely visible in the evening darkness. Rachel curled up in the crook of my arm, clutched her jacket collar at her throat, and stared at my face. I fixed my eyes at that spot on the rocks that I knew still carried glyphs from earlier times, held the phone to my ear with my right hand, and rested my head in my left. "Oh DeeDee, I'm so sorry. I'm so sorry."

The seconds I had to wait between the short sentences DeeDee tried to get out were nowhere near long enough for me to find the right words to console her. As my teeth started to chatter from cold and grief, I told her we'd come to Seattle as soon as we could.

"We love you," I said, lifting the receiver from my ear and hanging it up at the same pace as the sound waves that had inched between us. Still moving in slow motion, I folded Rachel into my arms as I told her that her childhood friend had just died. The friend she had known since birth who was just six months older and who had been in Stehekin with his family only four months earlier for Thanksgiving: that friend had ended his life. Rachel's sobs shook her body as she leaned into me.

We continued to hold each other as I again picked up the receiver to call Jerry at his mom's house. The distance between us felt immense. I hated that he was so far away, that he wasn't there to hold me, to hold us, and to reassure us that we would be okay. Comfort was hard to give and receive.

After I said a teary good-bye to Jerry, Rachel and I got in the car. I reached my right hand out to hold hers as I steered with my left, easing the Suburban back toward home. Stars sprinkled the sky, and the car hugged the curves of the road as if on autopilot. Rachel and I were silent, but questions pounded through my head. *How will I tell Matt his best friend killed himself? How will he respond? Might he try to kill himself? I have to make sure to hide the bottle of Tylenol that's in the medicine cabinet. I don't know how to do this.*

As we approached Ron Scutt's house, I saw a light was on. I needed help from another adult, and I couldn't think of anyone better than the kids' teacher. I tapped on the door, hoping I wasn't waking him, while at the same time hoping that if he was asleep, I would. I opened the door a crack and called his name.

"Ron, it's Iris and Rachel."

He leaned over the upstairs railing. "I'll be right down."

We three sat on the couch as the story of Nick's death stumbled out between my sobs. I don't remember anything specific that he said. I don't remember if he said he was sorry or if he asked questions about Nick and his family. I imagine he might have told us he remembered Nick from a summer visit, remembered Matt's story of the day he and Nick climbed to a perch at Rainbow Falls. And he probably said he was glad we had come to his house. I know whatever the actual words spoken, when they ran out, I felt ready to continue down the road toward home to tell Matt about his friend's death.

I found Matt sitting on his bed in his usual position with a book balanced on his knees.

"I have very sad news," I said as I squeezed next to him on the narrow twin bed. Rachel sat cross-legged near his feet. Matt's eyes widened while I told the story once again, as I would many more times in the coming days, never quite believing it. He was silent. If he had said anything that night, I would have remembered, but as usual, he kept his thoughts to himself. As we three huddled on the bed, I saw headlights in the driveway. Just as we all reached the foot of the stairs, Ron strode in through the back door. Though I'd worried earlier about interrupting his sleep, now I felt the same gratitude for his presence as when he'd welcomed Rachel and me to his living room.

"I'm sorry about your friend," he said, looking at Matt as he steered him toward the couch.

I turned toward the kitchen and motioned to Rachel. "Let's make some tea for Mr. Scutt, OK?"

Whatever Ron said to Matt has disappeared from my memory, but the image of the towering man stretching his arm over the small boy's shoulders remains. Rachel and I carried mugs of steaming mint tea for Ron and me and hot cocoa for both kids into the living room. We sat together, probably with long stretches of quiet sipping, as the fire crackled in the woodstove. Close to midnight, Ron said he needed to head home so he could get some sleep.

The next morning, the kids and I fixed breakfast and ate in silence.

"You know," I said, as they finished up the last of their granola, "you can stay home today if you want."

"I'd rather go to school," Matt said.

"Me too," Rachel said. "Mr. Scutt will understand if we're quiet today."

"OK," I said. "Let's get going."

Our farewells lasted a little longer than usual in the school's snow-packed driveway and ended with hugs instead of the customary wave. As I steered the Suburban toward home, I was wishing that I could just be at school being quiet, too. At Harlequin Bridge, I kept going straight instead of turning onto Company Creek Road. A few minutes later, I was choking out the story of Nick's death to Jean Vavrek.

"I just don't get it," I said to Jean between sips of the herb tea she'd made for me. A fire blazed in the cabin's woodstove. "Our families seemed so much alike. We shared childcare with each other, had regular potluck meals, and we went to Quaker meeting together. We've commiserated about not having any money and supported each other when we went back to school and started new jobs."

"It's hard when it hits so close to home, isn't it?" Jean said.

I closed my eyes, leaned my head on the couch, and let out a deep sigh. "If this could happen to them, it could happen to us."

"Iris, I'm so sorry," Jean said as she wrapped her arms around my shoulders. "Let your tears go. There aren't any words to take away this pain."

A couple of hours later, feeling spent from talking and crying, I again got in the car and turned toward home. I wondered how the kids were doing and what they were thinking. Were they scared? Sad? Confused? I wondered if they felt as I did that the world had stopped turning for a while. I didn't know yet how much it would hurt to see Jerry and DeeDee at their house and to hear their wails of grief when we went for the memorial. I didn't know yet that our friendship with Nick's family would never be quite the same, that we would never again be able to fully share with them the successes and joys of our own children. I didn't know then how many more times I would question why it happened to them, and why we were spared such tragedy. I also didn't know yet how often I would bargain with God to keep my children safe.

As the tires crunched over the snow on the approach to Harlequin Bridge, I did know that this was a lesson in trust. Ever since the flood, I never crossed the bridge without looking for the cedar that leaned toward the river. Today, the storm was inside me.

CHAPTER 19

Finding the Way Through

A S SOON AS THE SNOW MELTED ENOUGH that I could get to Boris' Bluff without skis, that's where I headed—Boris padding along behind me—for my own private Meeting for Worship. Channeling his tiger ancestors, Boris stalked through pine needles and scrambled over boulders that had rumbled down from mountain peaks over the centuries. I ambled, breathing in Ponderosa pines and Douglas firs reaching a hundred feet upward, breathing out three-journals-worth of questions about life, death, work and calling. At the tree trunk bases, saplings sprouted toward the lengthening days. Even though I'd exchanged tennis shoes for my winter boots, my feet still dragged with the weight of loss.

The distance between Stehekin and our downlake connec-
tions in Bellingham, Lopez Island, and Seattle never seemed
greater than in the days and weeks following Nick's death.
The annual Mud Flats celebration happened while we were
at Nick's memorial, and other harbingers of spring couldn't
penetrate the grief we carried with us when we returned. One
Friday in mid-April as Jerry and I drove to the school to pick
up the kids for the start of spring break, I cracked the window
of the Suburban. That familiar waft of warm air off the river
brushed my cheek, cuing the turn from the chill of winter. An
hour later, we all boarded the *Lady of the Lake* for the first leg
of another visit to Lopez, this time to visit the high school. We
spent the night with friends in Seattle and the next morning
drove two hours north to the ferry landing in Anacortes.

"Seems funny to drive a car onto the boat, doesn't it?" I said
to Jerry as we lined up behind a string of vehicles in Lane 1.

"Uh-huh," Jerry said, "but it's kind of nice to not have to
unload everything and lug it onto the boat."

"Also nice to know that if we missed this ferry, there'd be
another one in a few hours instead of in two days," I said.

"Doesn't look like we have to worry about that," Jerry said,
turning on the Ford's engine and following the orange-vested
ferry worker's waving signal to move toward the car deck.

"Can we go upstairs?" Matt asked as Jerry set the hand brake.

"You bet," Jerry said. "I'm ready to stretch my legs and check
out the view."

Although we'd made this trip several times over the years,
now I imagined what it would be like to call the San Juan Islands home. So much of it seemed different, yet familiar—the
boat's slow churn through icy water; shorelines much further
away than along Lake Chelan but still clothed in the perpetual

green of cedars, pines, and firs; the glacier-peaked Mt. Baker visible in the distance; the air, scented with salt and seaweed. Forty-five minutes later, as the ferry bumped into its berth, we all peered through the windshield up at the hand-carved wooden Lopez Island sign spanning the dock. Sunshine lit the curling bark on the Madronas interspersed among cedars lining the shore.

"Wow, no snow here," Rachel said as we joined a parade of cars down the center of the island toward the Ewert home. Driving down their long lane, I noticed tight yellow heads of daffodils swaying on four-inch tall stems.

On Sunday morning, Nancy rode with us to a home nearby where the Quaker Worship Group was meeting. With just a half-dozen or so people on the island who participated in worship, there wasn't a big enough group to support a Quaker meetinghouse. Yet, this small number had been gathering every week in people's homes for nearly a decade. That week's hosts, Polly and Steve, welcomed us to the small living room in their mobile home, just a few yards from the two-story house they were building. Like the Ewerts, and many others we would later meet, Polly and Steve had moved from place-to-place, saved to buy a piece of land, and soon would move into a permanent home. I felt a twinge of envy of our old friends, and these new ones, who were well-settled in the Lopez community.

As I fidgeted beside Jerry on the couch, I looked around the room at the faces of those who had gathered in silence that morning. I smiled at the thought of worshipping like this every Sunday and getting to know this small Quaker group. Soon, though, my mind whirred with sadness about Nick's death as well as thoughts about the coming days and months. I used every centering technique I knew to quiet the concerns about where we would live here, how we would support ourselves, and how the high school would be for Rachel and Matt. I sat up a little straighter and re-planted my feet on the floor. I tilted my head side-to-side, breathed in and out slowly, and rubbed my sweating palms across my thighs before bringing my hands to rest, open palms facing upward.

Soon after I shut out the questions about life on Lopez, new ones crept in. I brooded about what these nearly two years of sabbatical had taught me. Or hadn't. Why wasn't I clear about the work I was meant to do now? What about all those others who were burned out, disillusioned, and feeling helpless but couldn't take time like this to re-examine and renew? Why didn't I feel restored and ready to jump back into a life of activism and service? How could I even fret like this when I knew of so much suffering, especially of our friends who had just lost their son? I inhaled and exhaled again and again, listened for the gentle breathing of others in the room, and waited for wisdom.

Answers to some of my questions about Lopez emerged as the week went on. One day we took the kids to the high school to meet the guidance counselor. Compared to the Stehekin School, the Lopez kindergarten-through-twelfth grade collection of buildings sprawled like a small college campus. Between the school's parking lot and the main office, the kids listed all the things they wanted to find out from the counselor.

"It would be cool to play on a real soccer field again," Matt said as he tilted his head toward the field just past the south end of the high school building.

"I wonder if there's a girls' team," Rachel said.

An hour later, as we drove back to the Ewerts', the kids mapped out their first year of high school.

"I can't wait to take Spanish," Rachel said.

"What do you think about being on a co-ed soccer team?" I asked.

"Well, I've been the only girl playing soccer in Stehekin, so I guess I can play with the boys here, too."

"I want to take French," Matt said.

Rachel leaned her head against the backseat and smiled. "And can you believe there'll be about twenty kids just in the ninth grade?"

Another day I joined Polly and three other women to walk on the beach. Saltwater-smoothed pebbles spun out under our feet as the women asked about our life in Stehekin and told me stories of theirs on Lopez. I alternated between looking for colored sea glass and agates among the rocks and gazing at the expanse of water beside us. The snow-capped Olympic Mountains shimmered white on the horizon, so different from the sheltering V-shape the Stehekin Valley carved out of the North Cascades.

"Here, Iris," Polly said after pausing to bend down over the rocks. She placed a smooth, black stone the size of a walnut in my hand. "You see the way that white ring goes all the way around?"

I turned the cool pebble over, tracing the line that circled it. "It's beautiful."

"Rocks like that are a sign of friendship," Polly said. "Take it with you."

Over dinner our last night on Lopez, Greg asked the question I'd been mulling all week. "You're gonna' move here, right?"

"Yeah!" the kids shouted, in unison.

I looked at Jerry and raised my eyebrows. "Well, it seems like it would be a good place for us," I said, turning toward Greg. "We still have quite a few things to figure out, though."

"Like housing," Jerry said. "And we don't really know yet what we'll do about work."

"I'm hoping I can do more nursing consultation work," I said. "Should be easier to line that up here where I can have a phone and get set up for e-mail. But, that'll take a while."

"Aw, you guys will figure it out," Greg said, clapping a hand on Jerry's shoulder and turning toward the kids. "Hey Matt and Rachel, want to practice juggling clubs?"

While Greg, Jerry, and the kids cleared a spot in the living room for their juggling session, Nancy and I shuffled dishes from the table to the sink. With the open design of the main floor of their house, we could watch the show while we did clean-up.

"It would be so nice to have another Quaker family on Lopez," Nancy said as she scrubbed the lasagna pan and set it in the dish drainer. "Our worship group is great, but there are only a couple of us who have any experience with Quakerism outside of this group."

"I enjoyed worshipping with everyone on Sunday," I said. "We've had meeting occasionally in Stehekin, and I've been glad for that, but it's been more like a meditation group than Quaker meeting." I thought about the times a few Stehekin friends had sat with us in silence on Sunday mornings. They enjoyed the shared quiet, but no one seemed interested in learning about Quakerism. Afraid of appearing that I was pushing my beliefs on others, I hadn't volunteered information about Quaker peace activism or practices like the clearness committee. "I've discovered in Stehekin just how much I need solitude," I said as I dried the wet pan with the dishtowel, "but I also realize that I get something out of being with others in silence."

"Sounds like you've decided to move here," Nancy said.

"I think we're pretty sure. Now that the kids have learned about the high school and spent some more time here, I can't imagine them wanting to go back to Bellingham." I paused, watching them imitate Greg's movements and laugh as the striped juggling clubs sailed through the air and thudded to the floor. "There they'd be in a school with a thousand kids."

"And how about you?"

"I think Lopez would be a good fit," I said. I swallowed qualms about finding a place to live; that refrain was getting old.

Although spring hadn't arrived fully by the time we returned to Stehekin, the air off the lake had lost its bite, and the entire valley was free of snow. One day while the kids were at school, I dug in the closet for a couple of banana boxes we'd saved from a grocery order and filled them with our fleece-lined boots, the kids' snowsuits, and our cross-country gear. I knew to not pack up knit caps and gloves just yet; we'd seen the previous year that spring rains occasionally include an icy blast and a dusting of snow.

When Jerry brought the kids home that afternoon, I watched Matt bolt from the front seat, his jacket unzipped and flapping open. Rachel's pace was much slower, and her face had the dull look Ron had commented on in his report just before spring break: *I knew this would be a challenging semester for you. You're near the end of your Stehekin School experience, you're a single eighth grade young lady, you have been wading through water and snow for four full months, and you are surrounded by wild young boys who seem to literally be from another planet. Yes, these are big challenges for any young eighth grade student.*

I put my arm around her shoulder as she shuffled toward the house, her backpack dangling in her left hand and nearly brushing the muddy ground. "How was your day?"

All I heard was a sniffle in reply.

Matt stripped off his jacket and shoes in the mudroom, and seconds later I heard the sucking sound of the refrigerator door opening. "I'm going upstairs to read," he called, his words followed by the clomp of his feet on the carpeted stairs.

"Rachel, how about if I make us some mint tea?"

"OK," she mumbled, her backpack thudding to the floor. She sighed deeply as she unzipped her jacket.

"What's up?" I asked as I took our cups of tea over to where Rachel sat on the couch.

She held the steaming mug in her hands and stared at a spot on the floor. I could see her chin quivering as she turned her teary blue eyes toward me.

"I'm so sad about Nick," she said. "I just don't understand how he could kill himself."

"I don't get it either," I said. "But I know it helps to talk about it."

Rachel leaned into me and blew across the top of her mug. I stroked her hair and felt her body shake with the tears she let roll down her cheeks. Right beside the ache I felt for her was another one for my mom. She'd endured the loss of her husband much too young and had nearly lost her own life before she was forty. Memories of all those times she'd panicked about my travels, voiced fears about my safety, and worried about illness or injury made sense in a way they never had before.

And then, as if Rachel had heard my thoughts, she looked up at me. "I can't believe I won't see him again," she said. "It must be so sad for Jasmine and Jerry and DeeDee." She took a sip of tea and coughed. "And Matt won't even talk about it."

"Everybody handles their sadness in different ways," I said. "I know Matt misses Nick, too. I'm glad you can talk about how it is for you, though. I'm always ready to listen."

"Thanks, Mom," she said, setting her cup down and snuggling in closer. "I'll just be glad when school is over. I hope I can work at the bakery again this summer. Oh, but where are we going to live?"

"That's a good question. We're checking out some possibilities, but not Robbie's family's cabin," I said. "Somebody told us the Bowles cabin across from Libby's house might be available this summer.

"That would be cool, so close to Libby and the bakery."

"It's not definite yet," I said, "but I've got my fingers crossed."

In the weeks following our return from Lopez, the pace of life in the valley quickened in rhythm with the rise of the river from spring snowmelt and the budding of the trilliums. One of the earliest spring flowers in the valley, the trillium's three white petals nestled between three broad, forest green leaves encourage everyone to believe that winter really is over. The flower is such a cause for celebration that each year around Mother's Day, everyone gathers at the school for "The Trillium Festival," a kind of community talent show. When a sign-up sheet for acts appeared on the bulletin board at the post office, I wrote my name and Jerry's to read selections from *Poems for Two Voices*. Others had volunteered solos and duets on flute, piano, fiddle, and guitar, and Rachel and Matt planned a juggling routine.

In between house hunting and continuing to pack cold-weather gear we'd no longer need, I picked up my pace of making block print note cards and calendars for my final season in the Craft Cabin. By then I was partway through my fourth journal, filling another fifty or so pages with my almost-daily routine of morning free-writing. One day, after another session of scrawling doubts that God might be calling me to different work, might want me to live a more contemplative, creative life, I stashed my journal under the stack of books on my night stand and stepped into my walking shoes. Boris brushed past my legs as I opened the back door, his swaying gray and black tail beckoning me to follow. As he veered to the left behind the house, I knew we were bound for his bluff.

By now, this route into the forest was as familiar to me as the road that took us over Harlequin Bridge, along the river, past the school and the bakery, and to the landing. Still, I paused at times to savor the pine scent as Boris and I trekked deeper into the woods. I stopped to study the whorls of green lichen on the rocks and boulders that Boris led me past. Soon we arrived at the sloping mound that I'd climbed so often, sometimes when it was covered with snow, other times splattered with rain.

That day, I sat on the rock's highest spot, warmed by the sun breaking through the cottonwoods and pines on their ascent to the surrounding foothills and peaks. If not for the slice of sky visible through the canopy, you could believe the world ends right there. Once again, I breathed in the spicy, menthol scent. Boris coiled beside me as I wrestled with questions about nursing. Did my work make any difference? Could I stay in this system so driven by the budget ledger? Had I lost my compassion for those in need?

Boris' purr vibrated through the windless air. I craned my neck and stared at snowy peaks towering five thousand feet above, their ridges cascading in waves of purple beyond my vision. Unexpectedly, a familiar calm rippled through me, much like it had that night years earlier as I awaited results of the pregnancy test. I sensed that Boris and I weren't alone. All I heard was my own gasp of awareness of God's presence and an unexplainable feeling of connection with all people. The cement block of worry about the abused women and children, the struggling teen mothers, and the disease outbreaks lifted from my back. Tears welled as my inadequacy evaporated.

On Boris' Bluff, I grasped that I have my part to play, but it's not up to me alone. The carving effect of melting snow and ice, the rush of the river, the new growth after the forest fire taught me that the smallest touch, the briefest contact, the quietest diligence, can make a difference—can change the course of a river. There, I embraced both my smallness and my greatness. As the sun started its slow descent behind the ridgeline, my mountain-trekking tabby and I headed for home.

CHAPTER 20

Graduation

O NE DAY, standing in the lobby of the post office, I stared
at the window of mailbox number twenty-six. I could
hear the click, click of letters tapping against the glass as Don
sorted the mail into the boxes, and I stood up a little straighter
when I saw a white envelope pressed against the window of
ours. With all the planning under way for the summer, the kids'
graduation, and our pending move to Lopez, I hoped every
day's delivery would bring something for us.

"You better wait until Don's all finished," Jean said, noticing
my lean toward the row of mailboxes. "You know he doesn't
like it when we start grabbing mail before he's got it all in."

I rested back against the wall. "You're right," I said, "but I keep
hoping for a letter from the Bowles' about renting their cabin."

"OK, that's it for today," Don's voice called out.

Seconds later, Jean and I stood at our respective boxes, twisting the gold knobs to the numbers of the combinations. I reached in and pulled out a small stack of envelopes. There, in the upper left-hand corner of one, was the return address I'd been waiting for. My hands shook as I slid a finger under the flap and pulled out a letter.

"Woohoo," I hooted as I read through the letter from Steve Bowles. Jean came up behind me and peered over my shoulder. "We got the cabin," I said as I turned to hug her.

"No mosquitoes for you this summer," Jean said.

"And no pack rats, either," I said.

"Well, you never know about that," Jean said. "That place has been closed up for a few years."

Jean might be right, but her warning didn't dampen my relief as I headed home to tell Jerry the good news.

Just a few days earlier, Don had slid a letter from my mom into our mailbox. She'd written a "yes" to our invitation to her and Steve to attend the kids' graduation. I'd felt a mix of pleasure and dread that they were making the trip from California. Mom had voiced plenty of fears about our move to Stehekin, and I wasn't sure if her experiencing the reality of the place would ease or intensify them. With her acceptance letter in hand, I made a trip to the landing to work out some of the details over the phone.

"Got your letter," I'd said. "It'll be good to have you here for graduation." I paused to let my words make their way through the satellite transmission. "We'll check with the postmaster and his wife about renting their cabin while you're here."

"Well, whatever you think," Mom said. "We don't need anything fancy. But there'll be indoor plumbing, right?"

"Yes, it's a very nice place. I think you'll be comfortable." I paused again before launching in to directions about getting the boat in Chelan and where they should stay the night before.

"This sounds so confusing," Mom said. "Well, I'll bring a nice pot roast in the ice chest."

"You don't…" I started and stopped as I realized my mom had more to say.

"I know you can't just run to the store there in Stehekin, and I want to contribute something to the kids' graduation dinner."

"Okay, Mom," I said, not convinced that a hunk of beef that had traveled in a cooler from northern California to Stehekin was what we wanted on the menu. As I paused so my words could make their way to her phone receiver, I thought of how often she'd prepared special dishes for me. Report card day usually warranted a tin of her Tollhouse chocolate chip cookies after school. They'd also be waiting for me when I came home on breaks from nursing school along with lemon bars, a Pyrex-dish of lasagna, and green beans in cream sauce with canned onion rings sprinkled on top. Birthdays called for her choco-late sheet cake, and about one Saturday a month I'd wake to the smell of Pillsbury cinnamon rolls with white icing dripping down their sides.

Although Mom's idea of fresh bread was to buy unbaked baguette loaves that she browned in the oven, I understood her pleasure in filling the house with smells of butter, sugar, and cinnamon. One of the many rewards of our simplified lifestyle, combined with my growing skills as a baker, was to make whole grain breads and professional-looking pastries for family and friends. I looked forward to continuing my home baking once we left Stehekin.

Mom's voice broke through my thoughts about lemon bars and lasagna. "Is there anything else you want us to bring?"

"Might be good if you brought some Diet Pepsi," I said. "I know how much you and Steve like that, and that's not something we usually have on hand."

"Okay. Say, have you guys decided to move to Lopez?"

"Seems likely," I said. "We're going back there next weekend to check out a house we might rent. We'll..."

Mom's words ran over mine as she again forgot about the delay that made questions and answers collide when we didn't allow for the pauses. "What will you do..."

"... know more... go ahead, Mom"

"Oh hell, I hate this damn phone. What will you do about work there?"

"We've got some ideas. We'll fill you in more when you're here."

"I guess I'll just have to wait, then."

"Graduation will be here before you know it, Mom. Just write us a note if you have any questions about your trip here."

"ok. It'll sure be easier when you have a regular phone again."

Easier, maybe, I thought to myself as I drove back home. I conceded it would be nice to just drive to the store if we ran out of something, and talking on the phone with Mom wouldn't be so frustrating. Time would tell, though, how a return to the downlake world would affect my growing sense of how to lead a more balanced life.

Just as trilliums, buttercups, and glacier lilies burst into bloom, our final springtime in Stehekin brimmed with activity. The trip to Lopez resulted in a signed lease for a house half a mile from the school; back in Stehekin we started to sort belongings we'd need through summer and packed the rest to be loaded onto the barge in August.

We toured the Bowles cabin before committing to it start-ing right after graduation. "This place sure is close to the river," I said to Jerry as I looked out the window above the cabin's kitchen sink. Spring run-off from the snow in the mountains had turned the river into a bubbling swirl.

"Last year's flood ate away more of the bank, that's for sure," Jerry said. "Steve told me he's not sure how much longer they'll be able to keep the place because of the erosion."

"It just has to make it through the summer as far as I'm con-cerned," I said. I knew I sounded self-centered, but five moves in two years, plus a house search on Lopez, had shifted me into survival mode about our remaining time in Stehekin.

*   *   *

As eighth-graders, Rachel and Matt had stepped into the leadership roles reserved for the oldest students. Along with their grade-mate John, they served as "editors" of the newspaper the school produced each year. The students had studied calligraphy, and many of the paper's headlines were done with Matt's calligraphic flourish. His story about a hike with Mugs and his dad, Jonathan, made it into the paper, too. "Malicious Mac" recounted the trio's eight-mile climb to Mc-Gregor Mountain's 6500-foot summit. He'd conquered some other challenges that year, too. Ron's summary of Matt's second year at Stehekin School applauded his growing ability to listen as well as ask questions. He praised Matt's leadership skills and the example he set for the younger students. It would be a few years until Matt would express his own assessment of his time at Stehekin School.

"That's where I learned to love learning for learning's sake," he told me not long before his high school graduation.

Rachel's writings about the flood and the school trip to Horseshoe Basin were included in the school paper, too. Those pieces demonstrated what Ron had noted in his end-of-the-year letter to her: *It seems to me that when you go upstairs to write that you are engaging in a labor of love.* None of us could have known then that during her two years in Stehekin, Rachel's two passions—cooking and writing—were born.

The closing days of the school year centered on preparations for graduation. We'd attended the ceremony at the end of Rachel and Matt's seventh grade year and enjoyed the singing, recorder playing, and sharing of memories by families of the graduates, friends, and community members. That first year, Libby, the only eighth-grader, had received a quilt made by the entire school and many community members. The four of us had signed our names on fabric to be among the many hand-stitched onto the quilt by Roberta Pitts, the postmaster's wife. We'd seen some of these quilts in homes throughout the valley and knew they were given to graduates who had attended the school for five years or more. This year's graduates had been in Stehekin a shorter time, so we wondered what their community gift would be.

I wondered, too, how it would be to have Jerry's mom and my mom and Steve in the valley and at the graduation ceremony. This would be Florence's first time in Stehekin without Windsor. We decided to have her stay at our house since she was there alone. Mom and Steve would be at the Pitts' cabin, which included use of a van so they could get around independently. Since my mom's idea of camping had been to park our Winnebago motor home at a KOA campground, I knew she'd appreciate the privacy and comfort of Don and Roberta's well-equipped guesthouse across the river from our place. I wasn't so sure how she'd deal with hearing everyone refer to me as Iris and wondered whether that would fuel her sense of humor or her resentment.

"Welcome to Stehekin," we all shouted the day before graduation as Mom and Steve reached the end of the metal-grated walkway from *The Lady* to the landing. Mom's bright blue eyes glistened with tears as both kids wrapped their arms around her torso. Just like that airport greeting in Florida a dozen years earlier, they helped bridge the gap between my mom and me.

"Glad you're here," I said after the kids ended their embrace and I gave her my own.

"Me, too," she whispered into my ear before turning to Jerry for a hug from him.

"Hey Grandma," Matt hollered, "I see an ice chest with your name."

"I'll bring the Suburban down after everything's unloaded and we can pick up your gear," Jerry said.

"We should empty that ice chest as soon as we can," my mom said. "The roast is probably just about thawed."

"Good," I said. "I cut up potatoes, carrots, and onions to put in with the meat. I could stick it all in the oven for dinner tonight."

Florence offered to keep an eye on the dinner while we helped Mom and Steve settle in their cabin. We spent the rest of the afternoon on a short tour of the valley and ended the outing at Rainbow Falls. Spring runoff made the falls roar and left a chilling mist on our faces as we tossed our heads back to take in the cresting water three hundred feet above. I slipped my arm through Mom's as we walked among the cedars back to the Suburban.

"I can see why you like it here," Steve said that night at dinner. "It sure is beautiful."

"I know it wasn't easy for you to get here," I said, "but I'm so glad you got to see it firsthand." I looked around the table at Jerry, the kids, Mom, Steve, and finally, Florence. Her eyes teared as I said, "I'm glad we're all here together. And I know we all miss Windsor."

"Well, I wasn't going to miss eighth grade graduation for my only grandchildren," Mom said. "Nice job on the roast, Sta . . . honey."

"Thanks, Mom," I said, looking directly at her and smiling, with relief both that the pot roast didn't seem any worse for its journey and that she caught herself on my name. Out of the corner of my eye I could see the kids stifling giggles.

"Yes, Iris," Florence said, "everything is delicious."

On Saturday morning we all gathered again at our house for breakfast. The kids had requested cinnamon rolls and orange twists to start their graduation day, so I rose early to get the pastries ready. Soon after lunch, Jerry and the kids left for the school in Sir Arthur, and I drove Florence, Steve, and Mom in Colonel Mustard.

Just as for the previous month's Trillium Festival, the motion room at the school had been transformed. At the end of the day on Friday, the kids had moved the wooden desk chairs from the main classroom and folding chairs from the closet into the motion room and arranged them in rows like a theater. Ten chairs faced the audience along with the upright piano. By the time we arrived on Saturday, fresh flowers in vases sat on each windowsill. A table in the main classroom held a bowl of punch and a large carrot cake, its cream cheese icing decorated by Tammy with purple and yellow pansies.

As all of the kids stood to play selections on their recorders, my mind wandered. I knew from graduation the year before that there would be an opportunity for people in the audience to speak. Every time I started to think about what I might say, a jumble of memories and emotions lodged in my throat. I couldn't imagine that I'd be able to get out any of the words of pride and gratitude I might want to express without blubbering. And as I thought about what my mom might say, my heart pulsed a little faster.

Ron's voice broke through the one in my head as he said, "Now is the time people from the community can share memories or good wishes for our graduates."

I kept my gaze on Matt and Rachel as friends shared stories and spoke of their admiration of them and John. Recollections of Rachel monitoring the younger kids during recess and of Matt and Mugs performing a skit at the Halloween party brought chuckles from the crowd. When my mom stood, I saw Rachel and Matt look at each other. My damp palm gripped Jerry's hand.

"I'm Rachel and Matt's grandmother," she said, "and this is their other grandmother next to me. I must admit I wasn't too thrilled when Jerry and . . . um," she paused and looked at me, "when their parents told me they were moving to Stehekin." I nodded my appreciation for her again not using my former name. "It's a long way from California where I live," she went on, "and I never figured out how to talk to them on that satellite phone." She waited for the laughter that followed her admission to end. "But, I just want to say thank you to you, Mr. Scutt, and to everyone here for your teaching and care of them. I know this has been a good experience for Rachel and Matt, and I think it's prepared them well for their next steps. Thank you."

"That was nice, Mom," I whispered as she sat down. I looked at the kids and returned their smiles.

After a few more comments, Ron stood again and asked Roberta to bring out the gifts for the graduates. Steve stood with his video camera and recorded as each of the kids tore off the butcher paper covering on the packages and showed the audience what was inside—photographs of them, their class, and the school, surrounded by needle-pointed signatures of their classmates and teachers, all mounted on red fabric inside a cedar frame. Steve kept the camera rolling as Ron shook each of the kids' hands and posed for photographs.

The next day, we repeated the scene at the boat landing from two days earlier but in reverse, transferring gear for Mom, Steve, and Florence from our car to the loading area at the dock. After multiple hugs and tearful good-byes, all three of them took up posts at the railing around *The Lady's* open upper deck. It seemed strange to see Florence there without Windsor at her side. Jerry, the kids, and I stood at the landing, waving to Steve as he panned the video camera. Just as my mom had done whenever there was a departure, that day she continued to wave until she probably could no longer make out our figures.

CHAPTER 21

Wild Currents

THE RHYTHMIC THUD OF CLOTHES tumbling in the washer intruded on the morning quiet. Although the Bowles cabin was free of pack rats and mosquitoes, its elderly septic system couldn't handle the laundry of our family of four. Right after breakfast I'd loaded the Suburban with two baskets of wash, hoping to get to the public laundromat at the landing ahead of hikers and seasonal staff. Now, I steadied my journal on my knees and felt the sun warm my neck as I leaned back in my lawn chair, scribbling my morning pages while dirty jeans and shirts swirled in the machine.

I fingered the dark brown grain of the wooden pen resting on the page. When I'd bought it at the Craft Cabin our first summer in Stehekin, I'd hoped it would motivate me to develop a regular practice of journaling. Now I was nearing the end of my fourth, 9 x 12 book of blank pages.

I re-read what I'd gotten down so far that morning. I'd be-rated myself for a lapse in writing and wondered why I still felt so fatigued after nearly two years of a slower pace of life. Even though the previous weeks had been filled with the kids' gradu-ation and our move, this year's "hundred-day season" was just getting started. I'd had months of the slower, off-season rou-tines that allowed time for reading, cooking, skiing and hiking, playing games with the kids, writing, and block printing. Now I wondered if I should feel rested enough to return to full-time work in nursing or whether what I'd learned was how much I needed a balance among many interests and callings. As the bakery geared up to be open seven days-a-week, Jerry picked up more hours driving the shuttle for the Ranch, and both kids started summer jobs, I knew I'd have less time to ponder these lingering uncertainties.

Near the end of June, Jerry had a bout of diarrhea that made us suspect the sparkling water from our tap, pumped into the house directly from a glacier-fed creek, might be con-taminated with giardia. When Jerry's abdominal cramping worsened just as his bus-driving schedule intensified, he knew he had to do something.

"Give Mike a call and see if he'll prescribe something," I said one day when Jerry was working a split shift.

Mike was a family practice physician in Chelan. We'd met him, his wife Kerry, and their four children a few years earlier at a Quaker gathering and had stayed at their home during most of our comings and goings between Stehekin and downlake. It was their younger daughter who had guided Rachel through her first menstrual period at Junior Friends camp. Despite full lives with Mike's private practice, Kerry's teaching and playing violin, and their kids' music and sports activities, the entire family took off when they could for skiing and hiking. Stehekin, just a boat ride away, was one of their favorite destinations, and they were familiar with the community's remoteness. On more than one occasion, Mike had provided medical advice to ease access to care, so consultation with him seemed like the place to start with Jerry's current symptoms. Within a few hours of Jerry's call, there was a package waiting for him at the floatplane dock. Mike had phoned in a prescription to the pharmacy in Chelan and had the antibiotics delivered to Chelan Airways to bring on their next flight to Stehekin.

A few days later, Jerry called me in to the bathroom. He'd had giardia before and was surprised that he continued to have abdominal cramping even after being on the antibiotic; if anything, it had gotten worse. Now he was showing me bright red blood along with diarrhea stools in the toilet bowl. Here was another time that my nursing background was a liability rather than an asset. After twenty years working primarily with pregnant women and young children, my expertise in much of adult health was outdated. That, coupled with growing up with a mother who tended toward hypochondria, led me immediately to imagining this blood was a sure sign of colon cancer. I tried to keep those fears from my face and my voice.

"You need to go downlake to see a doctor," I said. "No more treating over the phone."

Had we lived downlake, a family doctor likely would have started more conservatively with a physical exam and a sigmoidoscopy, surmising that hemorrhoids were the source of this blood. Fortunately, though, the doctor Jerry saw in Chelan referred us to a specialist right away and saved us multiple trips and delays. Within a few days, Jerry and I were on our way to Wenatchee for his appointment with a gastroenterologist and a colonoscopy.

I accepted the gastroenterologist's invitation to remain in the procedure room as he advanced the scope through Jerry's colon. The mild sedation worked well; Jerry snored softly while I squinted at the screen. The lining of his colon looked like it was covered with canker sores. Although relieved there was no sign of cancer, seeing the mass of ulcers made my stomach burn.

"This is definitely some kind of inflammatory bowel condition, maybe Crohn's Disease," the doctor said. "I'll take a little sample so we can biopsy it."

I recalled my nursing school days caring for a teenager who'd been in and out of the hospital for years and had a large part of his colon removed because of Crohn's. I placed my hand on Jerry's shoulder and bit my trembling lip.

"I'll want to start him on a steroid," the doctor said as he withdrew the scope. "That will quiet down the inflammation and give the ulcers a chance to heal. Then we can switch him to another non-steroid anti-inflammatory medication that he'll probably need to stay on for the rest of his life."

"What about his diet?"

"Oh, it really doesn't matter what he eats. We think this is an autoimmune condition and that stress is more of an issue. These medicines will take care of everything."

Stress? After all the changes we'd made to have a simpler, less pressured life, how could that be the cause of these ulcers? And as much as I wanted to believe that Jerry wouldn't need to make any food changes, I couldn't imagine that what he ingested didn't have some impact on this part of his digestive system. With the possibility of an autoimmune disease, I already was thinking a naturopathic approach might offer some help, too. Once we lived on Lopez and had a phone and closer access to specialists, coming up with a plan for care would be easier. Hopefully these medications he'd start on now would bring him some relief for our last couple of months in Stehekin. After another night in Wenatchee, we returned home with a new prescription, consolation that there was no sign of cancer, and more than a few questions about future treatment.

By now, the tourist season and our schedules were in full swing. I alternated early morning baking shifts with some days working the counter. Rachel again supplemented dishwashing at the bakery with babysitting and cleaning at Silver Bay Inn, and Matthew spent most days at Ron's bicycle rental stand. Jerry was back to work driving the Ranch shuttle full-time, making multiple trips up and down the valley with guests from the landing, pies from the bakery, and gear and people going on river raft trips.

Once the wild currents in the Stehekin slowed a bit following spring run-off, Cliff's rafting guides offered regular day trips on the river. They'd put in the rafts at a spot near the Ranch and float the ten miles to the head of the lake. Our first summer in Stehekin, we'd accepted one of the free trips down the river that Cliff offered to locals; he used those runs as training for his guides. One day late in June, the four of us had wriggled into neoprene wetsuits and zipped up life jackets before climbing into a rubber raft with a couple other locals and a new guide and his veteran teacher. Icy spray bounced off the raft's sides and into our faces as we got the hang of paddling through the rushing water. My heart pounded as the raft dipped and turned through the currents and around boulders and tree branches littering the course. The Stehekin may have been classified as the least treacherous at Grade I or II, but I gripped my paddle as if each ripple was the approach to Niagara Falls. When I took my eyes off the turquoise churn long enough to look at Jerry and the kids, I saw grins spreading from ear to ear.

This final June in Stehekin, though, we passed on the ride down the river; between graduation, moving to the Bowles cabin, our unexpected trips downlake for Jerry's medical appointments, and working, there was no time for such an outing. Some afternoons when I was at home, I'd hear laughter and excited shouts a few minutes before I'd look out the kitchen window to see rafts jounce along the river's course. Jerry would hear the passengers' tales when he met them at the head of the lake and drove them back up-valley. The day after the community's Fourth of July festivities, two rafts floated the river to celebrate the fourteenth birthday of Autumn, a Stehekin girl.

Just the night before, we'd been with Autumn and other Stehekinites at the annual Iditardog; Libby and her family had started this competition for Stehekin dogs a couple of years earlier. Even people who didn't have dogs milled around the events in an open field across from the rustic "Libby's Lemonade" stand that she operated most days in the summer. Costumes for the dogs were encouraged, and Murphy didn't seem to mind the swim trunks and goggles we dressed him in. There were dogs in vests, hats, neck ties, and tutus, all of which they gradually shed as their owners led them through an obstacle course, urged them to leap into the back of a pickup, and tempted them with treats to sit, stay, and shake. At the end of the festivities, the humans cooled down with Libby's lemonade while the dogs lapped up icy river water from buckets and panted in the shade under the pines.

The next day, Autumn, her mom, and her sister, plus two nurses on vacation were in one raft with Steve Farmer guiding; the other boat held another tour guide, plus Chelsea and Reed Courtney, a niece and nephew of Cliff. Chelsea was a couple of years younger than our kids, and she'd been one of Rachel's allies dealing with those "wild young boys," such as fourth-grader Reed, at school.

About halfway through the float, the Courtney kids' raft slammed into a logjam at Buckner Hole, flipped over, and dumped them and the raft guide out. Jerry told me that night how he'd learned about the accident. As he'd waited at the landing to meet the rafting group, a floatplane touched down. By then, some of the witnesses to the accident had arrived and filled him in. I heard a catch in his voice as he related the story about these friends of our children.

People fishing in the river had seen the raft flip and had run to the nearby house of a Park Service employee who radioed for help. Reed and the guide kept their heads above water and someone, no one could remember who, pulled them out of the water. Chelsea, though, got caught under the jam. The story went that she remained trapped for seven minutes until Steve jumped on the logs to free her, and then he and the nurses pulled Chelsea into their raft. She had a thready pulse and wasn't breathing, so they started CPR and paddled to the riverbank. By the time the raft got to shore, a Park Service station wagon had arrived and a paramedic from Chelan was on the way in a helicopter.

At the scene, Carl, the paramedic, had looked at Chelsea's ashen face and slid a tube past her gray lips. Her arms and legs were motionless at her sides as Carl attached the breathing bag to the tube, squeezed air into her lungs, and glided her into the helicopter for transport to the hospital in Wenatchee. Reed, his mom Liz, and his aunt boarded the floatplane to Chelan, and a Park Service boat started to course down the lake toward Chelsea's dad, Tom, piloting the barge. I imagined the terror Liz must have felt as the helicopter lifted into the afternoon sun.

That night, we gathered at the community hall with almost everyone from Stehekin. Jerry and I scooted four chairs close together, Rachel and Matt sitting between us. I held Rachel's hand as people offered vocal prayers for Chelsea. I thought back over the many times I'd seen her smile at school events, during pickup basketball games on the school's outdoor court, and just the day before at the Iditardog. My prayers were silent and filled with questions as much as requests. What is to be learned from such a crisis? How do we find the balance between cherishing each moment and knowing life could be turned upside down just like a raft slamming into logs?

The next day, news filtered throughout the valley that Chelsea was stable and had a normal brain scan. Doctors surmised that the frigid river water had slowed her body functions so much that her brain hadn't been deprived of oxygen in those minutes before rescuers started CPR and the paramedic intubated her. Three days later she was walking, talking, and knew everyone around her. She couldn't, however, recall the details of the accident.

By the end of July, Chelsea had returned to the valley, amazing all of us with her apparent full recovery. Each re-telling of the rafting incident added to my reverence for the human body and the skills of those who care for it. As unaffected as Chelsea seemed then, I couldn't have imagined she would graduate from the Stehekin School and a downlake high school, then go on to college and become an architect.

I remained respectful of the river and its wild currents. We'd seen, heard, and felt its force less than a year earlier as it had re-shaped part of the valley. Now, we stood watch as it continued to eat at the bank outside our kitchen window. Each time the river rose, it took away more of the property; not much ground was left around the spot where the pump house and a cedar hovering over it, perched. Our water supply here was as precarious as that cedar, much of the grass, dirt and rock that secured its roots having been swept away.

One day, in the midst of a windstorm, I returned home from my weekly laundry chore at the landing. White caps ruffled the lake; trees along the road swayed, and I heard limbs crack. I was surprised to see Jerry's bike leaning against the front porch; I hadn't expected him to be finished with work until the bus run for the dinner crowd.

"Jer?" I called as I went in the house. "Are you OK?" I saw through the dining room window that he was standing next to the riverbank. Something looked different about that scene, but I wasn't sure what it was. I headed out the back door.

"You're home early."

"Yeah, Steve Bowles flagged me down when I drove by his house this morning. Told me he was worried that with all this wind, the tree had gone down."

That's when I realized what I was seeing. Or rather, not seeing. I followed Jerry's gaze down toward the river. The cedar that had been poised over the pump house now lay just inches above the water; a trail of skidded rock led to the tree's mass of torn roots.

"Wow, no wonder Steve was worried about the pump..." I jerked up my head and turned toward the right. The pump house. "Oh!" I gasped, then smiled. The little building that protected the pump that powered water flow to the house stood firm. Somehow the cedar had missed it on its tumble down the bank.

I looked into the swirl of water, the cedar's needle-shaped leaves reaching toward it, and offered silent thanks. We'd been spared again, and reminded again of the paradox of holding on and letting go. I prayed that this cedar wouldn't someday snatch a raft and spill its riders into the river.

CHAPTER 22

Another Way Through

SOON AFTER JERRY LEFT HOME to finish his bus-driving shift, the power went off; although our cedar had missed the pump house, another one somewhere must have crashed down on electric lines. This time the outage lasted only an hour, so I didn't have to worry about perishables in the fridge or an alternative to cooking dinner on the cabin's electric stove.

I did worry, though, about how this latest stress of the tree's near-miss of the pump house would affect Jerry's health. He always seemed to take life's ups and downs in stride. He was the one who buoyed me when I felt inadequate, strengthened me when I felt weak, and eased my fears. Now I wondered if his outward calm masked worries he bottled inside, worries that inflamed his intestines and had made him sick. He seemed to be responding well to the steroids, but I had to restrain myself from quizzing him every time he went to the bathroom.

That night, after the kids had gone to bed, I asked him how he was feeling.

"I'm doing better," he said.

"Any diarrhea?"

"No."

"Blood?"

"Nope. I'd tell you if there was." As we sat on the couch, he draped his arm over my shoulders.

I leaned into the warmth of his body and fought back tears. "I get scared that you wouldn't let me know because you don't want to upset me. Are you worried about this?"

"Not really worried, just curious about what caused it and how I'll manage it. It makes me wonder if Dad had something like this. He and Mom never talked about it, but I know he had digestive problems." Jerry squeezed my shoulder and kissed my forehead. "We'll figure it out."

One of the questions people usually asked when we told them of our move to Stehekin was how people got medical care; they couldn't imagine being somewhere without a doctor and so far from a hospital, and I'd worried about that, too. Now, as we prepared to move to another remote location, I knew there were risks with such limited access. But between Chelsea's rafting accident and the way the doctors in Chelan and Wenatchee worked together for Jerry's new diagnosis, I trusted his assurance that we'd manage.

"I know," I said. "But promise me you'll let me know if your symptoms get worse, OK?"

He kissed my forehead again and reached for my hand. "I promise."

The wind continued to rattle the cabin's windows and sway tree branches on the other side of the river. Before we went to bed that night, I double-checked that the flashlights scattered around the cabin all worked and that I'd set the battery-operated alarm clock for the next day's baking shift.

Memories of my final weeks working at the bakery blur with those of the many days there over three seasons. By this summer, I knew the routines, the recipes, and the techniques for the line-up of baked goods the Stehekin Pastry Company was famous for. Robbie never taught me to make piecrusts and still teased me when my pizza slicing went crooked, but I felt a part of the baking team. Donnalynn didn't return to the bakery, and as Robbie trained her niece and a couple of other women from the valley for future jobs as bakers, I happily accepted a part-time schedule with more counter shifts and their later start time. One thing I'd learned over the three summers of baking was that I didn't want to continue work that started pre-dawn. Soon after our move to Lopez, I would politely decline a job offer at the bakery there.

Even after two years in this tiny wilderness community, I still yearned for time to be alone. Boris' Bluff was no longer a short walk from my back door, so one day, while Jerry and the kids were at work, I rode my bike to the trailhead for Buehler's Bluff. I hadn't hiked there more than a couple of times since that spring day a year earlier when Jerry's brother and his family had visited. Today was much warmer, the July heat drying the pine needles on the trail and baking the ground to dust. Although a shorter course than the trail to Goode Ridge, the switchbacks here were steeper, and I inhaled whiffs of *ceanothus* as my breaths deepened. Even without Jerry to spur me on, within half an hour I made it to a point open to the sky and the head of the lake. Here I could see Silver Bay, and today, the lake hid all evidence of the mud flats where just a few months earlier the community had gathered to fly kites. Sunshine lit the water, turquoise blending into dark blue along the shore.

I found a grassy spot to sit and leaned against a rocky mound, its edges smoothed by eons of wind, rain, and snow. My gaze followed the length of the upper portion of Lake Chelan; its forested rock shoreline zigzagged just like the pattern of thoughts going through my mind. I realized that, like many searchers, I'd be leaving this valley with nearly as many questions about work and calling as when I'd arrived. But now, I felt more easy about the journey; I accepted both a direct course like the lake stretching below me, as well as the coves and narrows along its route. My voice broke into the silent air—"Thank you."

A few days later, our friends the Evergreens would travel up the lake for one more visit. This time, they'd bring with them a black, hard plastic box about the size of the bread loaves we made at the bakery. We four adults talked quietly in the living room and suggested that Rachel, Matt, and Jasmine take Murphy for a walk.

DeeDee held the box in her lap and pried open the lid. Although the funeral home had delivered Nick's ashes a couple of months earlier, this was the first time she'd opened the container that held them. All four of us blinked away tears as she undid the twist tie around the plastic bag and reached her hand into the stone-gray ash.

As often as I'd witnessed illness and death, I'd never seen cremated remains. They looked much like the crumbling rock and dusty soil on the trail to Buehler's Bluff. I dipped my fingers into the bag, too, and gasped softly as I felt the grit of what had once been our young friend's skin and bones.

After the kids returned from their walk, we explained we were going to take some of Nick's ashes to Rainbow Falls. Jasmine reached for Rachel's hand, and Matt perched on the arm of my chair.

"That's a good place," he said. "Nick and I had fun climbing on the rocks there."

Mist from the cascading water sprayed us as we stood on a rocky ledge at the base of the falls. One by one, we dipped a handful of ashes out of the plastic bag. One by one, we tossed them into the swirling green and blue pool. The rush of white glacial water from above muffled our sobs and relieved us of trying to speak. We huddled together, arms resting on shoulders and linked around waists, as the sprays of ash disappeared into the watery flow.

*   *   *

IN THE FOLLOWING WEEKS, we gradually packed away items that we knew we wouldn't use until we unpacked them again on Lopez. I made one more batch of chocolate chip cookie dough before boxing up the Kitchen Aid mixer. I planned menus and mailed a grocery list and blank check to Safeway for the last time. I went for one last skinny dip in the river and then packed away my beach towel.

I had long before completed the twelve chapters in *The Artist's Way* but had continued to write morning pages almost every day. I had finished Matthew Fox's *The Reinvention of Work* and re-read sections I'd highlighted and underlined. Now I moved those and other books from my nightstand into a box we'd take with us on the boat instead of with the bulk of our belongings on the barge; I wanted them nearby when we moved into the rental house on Lopez. I had only a few pages left in my fourth Stehekin journal—that one stayed beside the bed and would go with me in my daypack. Within a week of our move to Lopez, I'd write my first morning pages there in a new journal. A decade later, I'd return to Fox's words, plus those of others who understood the connection between work and Spirit, as I recognized that my search for balance continued, that seeking clarity about work I'm called to would be ongoing.

Although we knew plans were underway for a farewell community potluck, we scheduled a few dinners with smaller groups of friends. One of those was with Jean, Jonathan, and Mugs. Jonathan poured shots of his favorite single-malt Scotch for himself and Jerry; Jean and I sipped wine. While the kids skipped rocks into the river, we adults reminisced about other shared meals; Jonathan's coaching of the school's three-member cross-country ski "team;" and about warming our bodies in their hand-built, woodstove-heated sauna at the river's edge. I dabbed my eyes with a tissue as I thanked Jean for the afternoon she'd comforted me after Nick's death. Jonathan headed for a refill.

"Hey, what are you going to do with the Suburban?" Jonathan asked when he returned from the kitchen. "You're not taking it with you, are you?"

"Nope," Jerry said, "Sir Arthur and the Ford will be enough vehicles for us on Lopez."

"Well, it would be a great rig for hauling my portable saw-mill to work sites. What do you think of a trade?"

By the end of the evening, we'd negotiated swapping Colonel Mustard and the remainder of our woodpile for a quilted cover that Jean would make for our bed.

"Jean, I remember the wall hangings you made after kids from the Washington coast visited the Stehekin School and kids from Stehekin went there," I said. I'd admired the series she'd titled "Cultural Exchange" and the pieces' images of ocean and mountains. "Do you think you could do something like that on a quilt with that view downlake from Buehler's Bluff and a beach scene from Lopez?"

"If you send me a picture, I'll see what I can do." Jean took a sip from her wine glass and peered at me over the rim. "Hah!" I heard her familiar laugh. "Just don't expect it anytime soon. I won't be able to get to it before the winter... and I mean *next* winter."

"No rush," I said. "It's something we'll keep all of our lives. Besides, it'll last far longer than the woodpile and probably will outlive Colonel Mustard."

"In that case, maybe you should add something else to the deal," Jonathan said.

Jean looked at me and rolled her eyes. "Jonathan!"

*   *   *

MORE THAN ONCE AS I PACKED, I stopped to reflect on the two years we'd been in Stehekin. Even though we'd known our time there was limited, it had become home, and I'd felt like we were part of the community. How I would miss Maria's vigorous wave and wide smile when I saw her blue Volvo coming toward me on the road, or Wally's thumbs up salute and grunt when he passed me on my bicycle. Lopez was known as "the friendly isle" because of the tradition there of waving to passersby, so we were well practiced for our future community. But I knew it would take awhile for me to recognize the cars and drivers I passed and presumed that, unlike in Stehekin, there would be many I would never know.

Some days, Jerry came home from work to find me weeping on the couch. Usually, it was some memory or photo I was packing away that set off the tears. One day, my tears had dried by the time he walked in the door, but a scene from earlier in the day was fresh in my mind.

"I was heading out to the front yard to make sure we hadn't missed any tools or juggling equipment," I said, following Jerry as he went to the fridge for a cold beer. "Just as I was about to open the screen door, a couple of deer right by the edge of the road popped up their heads. I swear they were looking straight at me." Jerry smiled, then took a swig. "I looked back and said, 'Good-bye, deer,' and they scampered toward Libby's lemonade stand."

"Well, there'll be plenty of deer on Lopez. You know everybody there has to fence their gardens."

"Right. But then, I heard something, and here came a black bear sauntering into the yard. It didn't stick around like last summer when that bear played with the pop can outside the cabin. It just turned its head toward me, then ambled through the yard and headed next door like it was going to the river." I felt tears stinging in my eyes again and turned to Jerry for a hug. "It was like the animals were all making one last visit before we leave." Jerry set his beer on the counter and wrapped his arms around me.

*   *   *

Early in August, as I unpacked our last order of groceries from Safeway and put the wilted lettuce in the refrigerator, I realized I was looking forward to doing my own shopping again. As much as I appreciated Alice's careful selection of not-too-bruised bananas and not-too-ripe avocados, I felt ready to navigate the grocery aisles and, in the summer, shop at the Farmers' Market. Soon we'd reclaim our furniture and other household items we'd stored in Bellingham and would have them in our house on Lopez. A house with a year's lease that we wouldn't have to move out of the next summer. And a group of people who met every week for Quaker worship.

Those thoughts were far from my mind, though, at the community potluck just a few days before our departure. There were no big speeches or teary good-byes, just lots of good food, laughter, and talk about when we would visit again. People in Stehekin went through this ritual repeatedly with the rotating population of seasonal Park Service employees and staff for all of the businesses that operated during the "hundred-day season." And there were the families like the Barnharts who moved downlake in some configuration or another so that kids could go to high school and someone stayed behind to work and take care of Stehekin property. In a year, Jean and Mugs would be part of that migration when Mugs started high school in Chelan and Jonathan stayed behind in Stehekin. There were some retirees, too, who left for warmer, less snowy climates in the winter. And, there often were families like ours who came to Stehekin for a year or two and then moved on. Although people at the potluck were experienced with these shifts in the population, I suspected that the laughter and the abundant food were part of their coping with the comings and goings of friends and family.

*   *   *

A FEW DAYS LATER, the *Lady of the Lake*, its white body trimmed in crisp blue, waited at the landing. We'd already said our good-byes to friends, knowing that most people would be at work. Captain Wilsey (now Kenny to us) sounded the boat's warning signal that it would leave in ten minutes.

The Lady's aluminum gangplank squeaked and creaked as we tromped across its grated metal one more time. The crew tossed our bags and boxes—bits of our world in Stehekin—into the cargo hold on the boat's lower deck. Sir Arthur, its covered bed packed to the roof, was already on its way to Chelan on the barge, along with a pallet of shrink-wrapped moving boxes bearing our names.

Today, it was Rachel's turn to make the trip downlake on the floatplane, this time along with Murphy, Skoshi, and Boris. Matt had boarded *The Lady* ahead of us to get a seat by a window.

The late August air was still and warm as Jerry and I leaned against the railing on the boat's upper, outdoor deck. I looked back toward the diminishing valley, the houses at Silver Bay growing smaller and looking even more dwarfed by the peaks of Buckner, Booker, and Boston. Beyond them I knew lay Horseshoe Basin, Agnes Gorge, Sahale Glacier, and McGregor Mountain. A sob escaped from my throat as Jerry and I embraced.

We spent that night with the Travers in Chelan. The next day, we repeated in reverse order the steps we'd followed two years earlier. This time, Sir Arthur waited for us at Tom Courtney's downlake barge company headquarters. We unloaded the shrink-wrapped boxes into a rented trailer and hitched it to the Tempo. Our caravan—the kids, cats, and I in the Tempo and Jerry and Murphy in Sir Arthur—snaked from east to west, this time over the North Cascades Highway and Washington Pass. Radio reception there was no better than on the approach to Stevens Pass. With the kids dozing in the backseat, I welcomed the quiet.

Eight hours later, we rolled up to the ferry terminal in Anacortes in time for the last sailing of the day to Lopez Island. The ferry's white body and dark green hull shimmered in the early evening light. As I inched the car onto the ferry's deck, I looked up toward the wheelhouse and saw the vessel's name on a wooden sign—*Chelan.*

I don't live in Stehekin anymore, but it lives in me—and in Jerry, Rachel, and Matt. It lives in the memories of black bears playing in the yard, forest fires, record-breaking floods, day hikes and cross-country skiing in the backcountry, star-filled skies, and the kind of quiet you only find far from traffic-filled highways. We remember laughing, crying, waving to, dancing and singing with, and being fed by the people in the Stehekin Valley. People who many times generously shared their knowledge, skills and kindness, as well as trucks, chainsaws, and pushes out of the snow. What lives on the most is what was not in Stehekin —the drive to always move faster and the unrelenting press to consume that dominates life "downlake." It was the absences—of television, phones, shopping malls, high-speed highways—that encouraged, and sometimes forced us to look inward. We reclaimed the joys of reading, letter-writing, listening to and playing music, face-to-face conversations with neighbors, hanging laundry on the line, walking and bicycling, and baking bread. We learned new ways to entertain and express ourselves such as knitting, juggling, writing, woodworking, and block printing. Far from feeling deprived, we found over and over again the riches of attending to what's truly important.

We never did go back to the old house in Bellingham; instead, we sold it a year after we moved to Lopez and bought a place there. My mom and Florence died one week apart in 2004, and Murphy died three weeks later. Skoshi and Boris are gone, too. Jerry's Crohn's Disease is in remission, and after nearly fifteen years working for the county Public Works Department, he's returned to his first career as a sign language interpreter. Matt and Rachel graduated from Lopez High School and went to college, hiking their own trails with partners at their sides—Rachel following her passion for cooking and self-sufficiency, Matthew (as he now prefers to be called) working as a French and Mandarin interpreter. Jerry and I continue to worship weekly in silence with the Lopez Quaker meeting, and more than once we've turned to them to help us discern God's leadings.

Since moving to Lopez, I've worked as an independent health consultant and a school nurse, gradually shifting most of my attention to writing. I've filled stacks of blank journals, and I've hand-bound hundreds more—some that include my original block prints—for sale in art galleries. I open one now and take out that wooden pen hand-turned by Don Pitts, the postmaster who placed a welcoming note in our Stehekin mailbox. My long-practiced urges to control, to protect, and to seek approval re-surface in my mind and on the page more often than I'd like.

Sometimes the wisdom I gained in Stehekin seems to fade. At those times, I climb the saltwater-lashed cliffs of Iceberg Point with my yellow lab/shepherd mix, Buddy. I sit among firs, their wind-twisted trunks bowed toward the ground, and imagine the Coast Salish people of the past, fishing for salmon and gathering gin-scented juniper berries after journeying "the way through" the Cascades. Here I continue to seek—not escape, but my own way through, listening for God's presence as I learned to do in those times of nakedness in Stehekin.

Acknowledgments

Portions of this memoir have been published previously as personal essays:

"Singed." *The Examined Life: A Literary Journal of the University of Iowa Carver College of Medicine*, Issue 5.1, October 2016

"Leanin' Into It." *The First Day*, Winter 2014

"Boris's Bluff."
   Oregon Quarterly, Summer 2013.
   First prize in Northwest Perspectives Essay Contest, Student Category, 2013
   Wildness: Voices of the Sacred Landscape, Anthology, Homebound Publications, June 2016.

"Eat Dessert First." *Alimentum*, July 2013.

"Hiking Naked." *SHARK REEF*, Summer 2011.

"Finding the Way Through." Essay included in anthology *Enlivened by the Mystery: Quakers and God*, Friends Bulletin Corporation, 2009.

"Mail Order Groceries." *Home Cooking*, March/April 2003.

"Rolling Old River." *SHARK REEF*, June 2002.

"Finding the Way Through." *Friends Journal*, November 2001.

Thank You

Many writers talk of the nature of this craft as being lonely; we describe solitary hours with pen on paper, fingers on keyboard. Even those who spin out stories in bustling coffee shops or on crowded buses tell of feeling alone as they block out conversations and activities surrounding them. It's on pages like this, though, where we acknowledge the people—typically in numbers rivaling a small-town population—who have accompanied us through the rough drafts, the revisions and re-revisions, the doubts about whether we have anything to say, and yet more revisions.

Even before I called myself a writer, a writing community started to form around me. Among the first was the late Tom Mullen and participants in his writing workshop at Pendle Hill Quaker Center. I thank them for opening me to view writing as my work. I returned from that workshop to the support of a writing group that I continue to meet with weekly: Suzanne Berry, Brooks, Marty Clark, Kathy Holliday, Rita Larom, Ann Norman, Lorna Reese, and Gretchen Wing. Rita and Lorna were there from the beginning fifteen years ago, along with Amalia Driscoll and the late Leta Currie Marshall. These long-time writing companions, along with Karen Fisher, Kip Robinson Greenthal, Helen Sanders, the late John Sangster, Alie Smaalders, and Migael Sherer have helped me transform "shitty first drafts" into essays that have made it into journals; shape experiences and memories into a book.

Quaker communities in Seattle, Bellingham, and Lopez Island, WA keep me grounded in my spiritual journey. In particular, several Clearness Committees have helped me discern leadings about work. Ever since I met Mickey Edgerton at a Quaker picnic thirty years ago, she has sustained me with her spiritual friendship, humor, and the reminder: "Oh, it's going to be a good day. There were tears before noon."

Countless writers shared their expertise and offered critique at workshops and conferences; thank you to Matthew Goodman at the Orcas Island Writers Festival for first suggesting I write a narrative rather than an essay collection. And to Scott Russell Sanders for encouragement about telling stories about happy marriages.

Credit for the title *Hiking Naked* goes to the "Flick Creekers" who have cheered me on for over a decade during annual writing retreats in the North Cascades and on Molokai. A special thank you to Amanda, Claudia, Karen, Liz, and Tee for your steadfast enthusiasm.

When I recognized I needed a push to reach my goals as a writer, the Whidbey Writers Workshop Master of Fine Arts program was there. It filled in my literary and craft gaps and broadened and deepened my writing community. Without exception, my classmates took seriously the program's value to help each other be the best writers we can be. Those who went above and beyond that call include Janet Buttenwieser, Jackie Haskins, Chels Knorr, Deborah Nedelman, YiShun Lai, and Andy Seiple.

This memoir is due in no small measure to Ana Maria Spagna. It's clear that forces beyond me brought us together, first as friends in Stehekin, and later as writers. She's been teacher, mentor, thesis advisor, and midwife with the patience, wisdom, and compassion worthy of sainthood.

When I learned about Homebound Publications and its commitment to "contemplative literature," I suspected I'd found the right home for my memoir. Luckily, founder Leslie M. Browning agreed, and I remain grateful for the hard work, caring professionalism, and integrity of Leslie and her independent press.

Thank you to the Stehekin community for welcoming my family and me. The people, and the place, continue to inspire me.

None of this would have been possible without the love, encouragement, and support of my family. Thank you, Rachel and Matthew, for being willing adventurers throughout childhood and ardent supporters in adulthood. Jerry, there could be no better companion on life's journey. I can't thank you enough for being at my side through all of the switchbacks, skinny dips, and seeking.

About the Author

Iris Graville is the author of *Hands at Work: Portraits and Profiles of People Who Work with Their Hands*, recipient of numerous accolades including a Nautilus Gold Book Award, and *BOUNTY: Lopez Island Farmers, Food, and Community*. She also serves as publisher of *SHARK REEF* Literary Magazine. Iris lives and writes on Lopez Island, Washington.

www.irisgraville.com

HOMEBOUND PUBLICATIONS

Ensuring that the mainstream isn't the only stream.

At Homebound Publications, we publish books written by independent voices for independent minds. Our books focus on a return to simplicity and balance, connection to the earth and each other, and the search for meaning and authenticity. Founded in 2011, Homebound Publications is one of the rising independent publishers in the country. Collectively through our imprints, we publish between fifteen to twenty offerings each year. Our authors have received dozens of awards, including: *Foreword Reviews'* Book of the Year, Nautilus Book Award, Benjamin Franklin Book Awards, and Saltire Literary Awards. Highly-respected among bookstores, readers and authors alike, Homebound Publications has a proven devotion to quality, originality and integrity.

We are a small press with big ideas. As an independent publisher we strive to ensure that the mainstream is not the only stream. It is our intention at Homebound Publications to preserve contemplative storytelling. We publish full-length introspective works of creative non-fiction as well as essay collections, travel writing, poetry, and novels. In all our titles, our intention is to introduce new perspectives that will directly aid humankind in the trials we face at present as a global village.

WWW.HOMEBOUNDPUBLICATIONS.COM